# The Parent's Guide to the Modern World

*The indispensable book for every parent of teens or soon to be teens*

By Richard Daniel Curtis

Illustrated by Paul J Smith & Maggie Qiu

© 2018 Richard Daniel Curtis

All rights reserved

First edition published 4/17

Second edition published 7/18

ISBN 13: 978-1-912010-12-7

Ebook ISBN 13: 978-1-912010-13-4

Published by: TKC Ltd

For more details on Richard's work, please go to www.richarddanielcurtis.com

# The Parent's Guide to the Modern World

Richard Daniel Curtis

# Table of Contents

| | |
|---|---|
| Foreword | 1 |
| Introduction | 7 |
| Part One - Brain development | 13 |
|   The Brain | 15 |
|     Prior to birth | 17 |
|     The Early Years And Childhood | 18 |
|     Pre-adolescence | 19 |
|     During Adolescence | 20 |
|     After Adolescence | 22 |
|   Social And Emotional Development | 23 |
|     Self-identity | 24 |
|     Recognising The Rights Of Others | 31 |
|     Interacting With Others | 37 |
|     Recognising The Needs Of Others | 39 |
|     Reforming Sense Of Identity | 41 |
|   Having Difficult Conversations | 45 |
|     Information Giving Conversations | 47 |
|     Problem Solving Conversations | 49 |
| Part Two – The Parent's Guide to the Modern World | 53 |
|   Social Lives, Community And The Wider World | 55 |
|     Peer Pressure | 55 |

|   |   |
|---|---|
| Gangs | 60 |
| Knives And Weapons | 65 |
| Drugs | 71 |
| Gender | 85 |
| Sexuality | 89 |
| Terrorism | 93 |
| Radicalisation | 97 |
| **Phones** | **101** |
| Smartphones | 103 |
| Instant Messaging And Chat | 110 |
| Instant Broadcasting (Livecasting) | 117 |
| **The Internet** | **121** |
| Blogs | 122 |
| Collaborative Sites | 126 |
| Pornography | 128 |
| Hacking | 133 |
| Pirated Software, Music And Films | 139 |
| The Dark Web | 142 |
| The Internet of Things | 145 |
| **Social Media** | **149** |
| Trolling And Online Bullying | 151 |
| Facebook | 156 |
| MySpace | 161 |

| | |
|---|---|
| Twitter | 164 |
| Pinterest and Instagram | 168 |
| Immersive Technology And Experiences | 171 |
|     Virtual Reality | 171 |
|     3D Printing | 175 |
|     Brain-Computer Interfaces | 178 |
|     Interactive Eyewear | 181 |
|     Speech Recognition | 185 |
|     Gesture Recognition | 189 |
|     Gaming | 193 |
|     Holograms | 200 |
| Robots | 203 |
|     Artificial Intelligence | 208 |
|     Drones | 211 |
| Part Three – Helping Your Child To Succeed In The Future | 215 |
| General Rules For Technology | 219 |
| Skills For Tomorrow's World | 221 |
| Education | 222 |
| Jobs | 224 |
| Self-Awareness | 226 |
| Finances | 228 |
| Attitude To Technology | 229 |
| Interacting With Others | 231 |

| | |
|---|---|
| Key Points | 233 |
| Part Four – Glossary | 235 |
| About the Author | 245 |

# Foreword

The Parent's Guide to the Modern World

# Foreword

Growing up in a little town in South Carolina, I was fortunate to have a mom who pushed me to succeed. My mom was (and still is) my biggest mentor. She saw potential in me that I did not see in myself at the time, and I would not be standing here today without her support and guidance. If she was not such a big force in my life, especially as a teenager, I may have had the same fate as my peers who struggled with drug addiction and alcoholism, some still to this day. My mom showed that she understood me, and just that little bit of trust and understanding made the biggest difference in my life as a teenager.

Now, as a father of three sons, two of whom are teenagers, I try my hardest to support them as my mom did for me. I try to meet them at their level and understand where they are coming from so I can help guide them to where they need to be. Parenting teenagers is a tough job at times. In fact, I can honestly say it makes winning three Super Bowls in the NFL look easy!

# The Parent's Guide to the Modern World

There is so much to learn and know as a parent, and the advent of technology has drastically changed parenting. In some ways, making it even more challenging to help guide your child through adolescence. Teenagers have always faced societal pressures as they try to fit in with their peers. They must learn the right ways to manage the typical pressures and social anxiety that come along with adolescence, while dealing with social media pressures, bullying, weapons, and gangs. The availability of material online on these topics is extensive. Some of it can be instructive, but some can be harmful. Therefore, it is important to be able to help them learn how to effectively sort through this information.

I hope that as a parent, you will not run into every one these issues with your teenager, but there will be a couple situations that will resonate with any parent given some of the issues that their children come home with and the battles that they face every day. We all want to make sure that our children grow up to be healthy adults who make good decisions. It is important that we understand a little bit of the mechanics behind some of the decisions our teens face and how we can handle these situations better to help raise happy healthy kids into adulthood.

While nothing takes the place of great parenting, this guide gives insight as to how to better parent. It not only explains your teenager's brain and development, but offers practical solutions for some of the challenges we face as parents; whether it's about talking to your teens

# Foreword

about overusing technology, spending too much time on their smartphones, dealing with drug use or getting mixed up in other harmful things. It provides you with the tools to better understand why they feel how they do and how to address some of these issues in a much more thoughtful and emotional way. This will ultimately result in more effective parenting and help you guide your teens down the right path, like my mom did for me and like I try to do for my own kids.

*Troy Brown*

Father of 3 and former New England Patriot and 3x Super Bowl Champion

# Introduction

# The Parent's Guide to the Modern World

# Introduction

The 21st century is a scary time for parents to be raising children. Technology is advancing at a tremendous rate and society around us is changing on a daily basis. Now, unlike at any time, there are threats for children inside their family homes, as well as in the community. Parents feel like they have to monitor their child's every action. They worry about what their child is up to in their bedrooms far more than what they do when they are playing with their friends in the park, but then they are accused of being over protective.

Things humans only ever dreamed of are now a daily part of reality. New technology is emerging every day and the world is changing as a result. Computers have moved from being one per house, to multiple devices around the house and in pockets. Even the most technologically minded parents are struggling to keep up to date with the technology that their child is using.

The boundaries in society have shifted, for example, it is accepted that celebrities are now accessible. With just a few taps on the computers in someone's pockets, they can find out what their favourite actress had for dinner and where they go for their daily jog. In fact, with very little effort, it is possible to send them a message and there is an increasing likelihood that they will reply. Privacy as people know it is coming to an end.

The way humans communicate with each other is also changing. It was only a few years ago that there was one phone line in the house and families were queueing to use it at peak times. Nowadays, many young people do not even consider having a phone line installed as they are far more used to being accessible via the device in their pockets. This has had an effect on society's expectations of contacting each other. Immediacy is the watchword; people are expected to be contactable immediately and in return, they expect to receive information immediately. Employers even provide staff with technology that facilitates their ability to send their staff emails to read late at night or early in the morning. Although, in France a law has been passed recently to give employees the right to disconnect and ignore these out of work emails.

People socialise differently in the modern world. Social media allows friends to keep up to date on the relevant (and sometimes irrelevant) events in the lives of their friends. The conversations people have when they see friends now are very different and there is almost an

# Introduction

unwritten expectation to have read their posts or their blog. Likewise, the gap between seeing friends is widening as they're able to keep up to date with their news and react to it by pressing 'Like' on their latest post. Technology gives society a lot more immediacy when interacting with friends, but also a greater distance at times too.

People's working lives have had to change: the speed at which employees process things has increased as technology has advanced, and many tasks are being automated. There is an expectation of a lot more immediacy in actions and reactions. Employees are expected to be completing tasks whilst monitoring busy inboxes at the same time. They are expected to know information and reply to requests and demands with greater immediacy. There is an inherent expectation to daily lives that people multi-task well at all times of the day. It is common for people to be answering something on their smartphone at the same time as having a conversation without even an eyebrow being raised nowadays.

Those that have children have to not only learn all of these new skills themselves, they have to try and keep ahead of their children and what they are up to. May young people talk to their parents about technology the adults only vaguely know about, and adults are completely unskilled at helping them make safe choices about this new technology.

Therefore, that is why this book was written, as a guide to the 21$^{st}$ century for parents struggling to understand it themselves. It is not a book written to be read cover to cover in one sitting; a parent's life is too busy for that. Instead, it is a guide to the various things that parents will encounter to pick and choose from. The contents are certainly not exhaustive and, as with anything of this nature, there will be new technologies that are released.

The book is split into four parts. Part 1 focuses on a child's social, emotional and brain development from the womb until adulthood. Part 2 gives advice on various aspects of life in the 21$^{st}$ century. Part three gives ideas about things parents can be doing to help prepare their child for the future, and finally part four is a handy glossary for any parents struggling with the phrases their teen is using.

*Richard Daniel Curtis*

March 2018

# Part One - Brain Development

# The Brain

**Parts of the Brain**

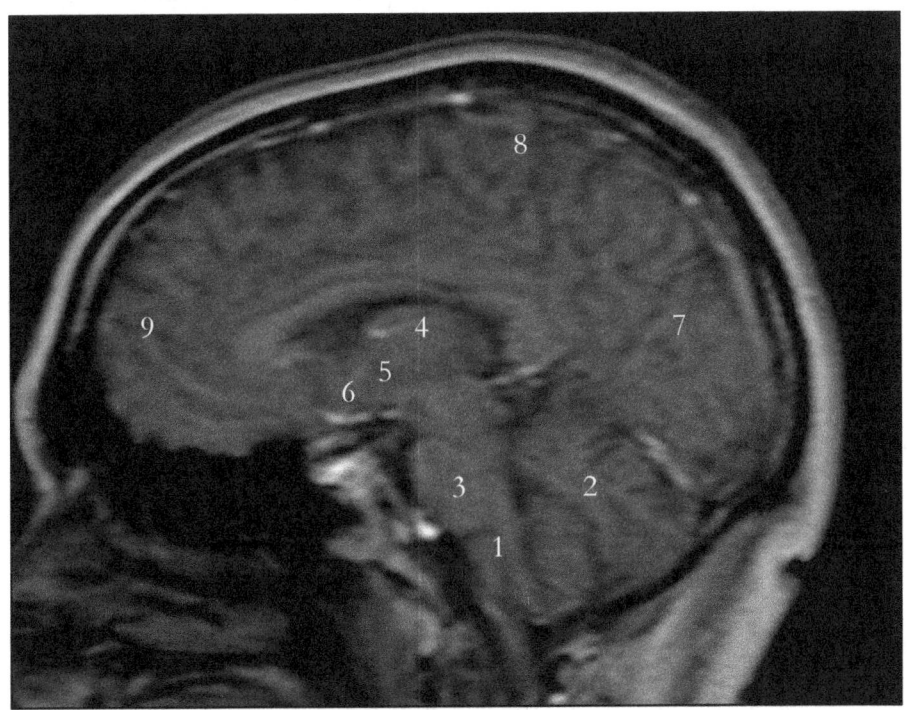

**Reptilian Complex** (Reptilian Brain)

>**Medulla Oblongata** (1) - Regulates bodily functions like pulse and breathing rates.

>**Cerebellum** (2) - Controls balance and voluntary muscle movement.

>**Pons** (3) - Connects both halves of your body to integrate movement like walking, running or swimming.

**Limbic System** (Mammalian Brain)

> **Thalamus** (4) - This is the area of the brain that receives all information from the body (apart from smell) and sends it to the right part of the brain.
>
> **Hypothalamus** (5) - The area of the brain that controls our drive and emotional and sexual responses.
>
> **Amygdala** (6) - This is the part of the brain that links senses to an emotional significance (like hot soup on a cold day) and help mediate aggression (physical and sexual), plus is involved in triggering fear.

**Neocortex** (human brain)

> **Occipital lobes** (7) - Controls visual perception and some aspects of reading.
>
> **Parietal lobes** (8) - Controls tactile (touch) and spatial perception.
>
> **Temporal lobes** (not shown) - Controls memory, musical awareness, sequencing, language comprehension.
>
> **Frontal lobes** (9) - Controls attention, motivation, initiation, personality, social behaviour, judgement, decision making, problem solving, and expressive language.

## Prior To Birth

As a foetus develops, the three parts of the brain develop: the reptilian (or hindbrain), the mammalian (or midbrain) and the future human brain (the forebrain). These are formed within the first month of pregnancy and are followed by the development of the *Medulla Oblongata* and the start of other regions, such as the *Cerebellum*, the *Pons* and the *Neocortex*. During the fifth week, the developing brain also begins the process of folding into the shape it will eventually develop.

The development of the brain continues throughout the remainder of the pregnancy, with the neurons migrating into the final positions during the two latter trimesters of pregnancy. The process of refining the brain cells that are required also begins at this stage and continues throughout childhood (a process called *apoptosis*). *Synaptogenesis* then begins; this is the process of creating, then strengthening (*myelination*), the connections between brain cells. This continues throughout childhood and is revisited during adolescence (see below).

# The Early Years And Childhood

The bonding a baby experiences helps with the connection and strengthening of different parts of the brain. As they experience new activities and games, different parts of their growing brain are fired up. This tells the brain that these neurons are needed and to connect them up. The more these activities are revisited, the more the conductivity to them is strengthened. Unused neurons are lost as our brain ruthlessly axes the ones that have not been activated. It then focuses on further *myelination* of the remaining brain cells as the growing child learns behaviours and achieves social competence.

## Pre-adolescence

In the two or three years leading up to puberty (roughly aged 10–12) the brain develops millions of new neurons, particularly in the *pre-frontal cortex* (the area at the front of the brain) and the grey matter surrounding it. Just as with the young child, it is important that these new neurons are used and so for the young adolescent this is often a period of trying new hobbies, activities or new experiences in order to ensure that these connect to the existing brain structure. Many parents are not aware of the importance of this period in brain development and so may miss this opportunity. This period is commonly referred to as the 'use it or lose it' stage of brain development.

## During Adolescence

Throughout puberty (approximately 13–15), the brain effectively shuts down the frontal lobes whilst it rewires. It begins work at the back and works forward, eventually seizing the opportunity to effectively reduce the working capacity of the frontal lobes, as it hard wires in the new neurons utilised in the previous growth stage and then culls the unused neurons. The frontal lobes are the region that controls personality, behaviour, risk analysis and our value system.

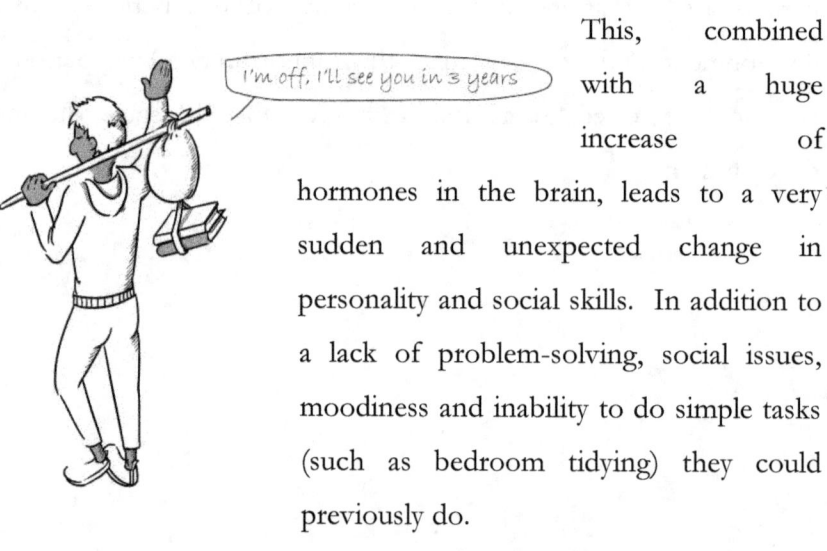

This, combined with a huge increase of hormones in the brain, leads to a very sudden and unexpected change in personality and social skills. In addition to a lack of problem-solving, social issues, moodiness and inability to do simple tasks (such as bedroom tidying) they could previously do.

There is an increase in risk-taking and emotion-based behaviour as the *amygdala* responds without the guiding voice of the frontal lobes. Demands or questions of the teen will often be perceived by the mammalian brain as a threat and will result in a confrontational response or refusal. Stress levels increase the *cortisol* level in the brain (and vice versa). Problems, chores or learning, which the brain could previously cope with, now present more stress for the teenage brain as the frontal lobes dealt with those in the past. Their brain craves stimulation and reward, so there is an increase in television, gaming, mobile phone and computer use. The frontal lobes are the region of the brain that processes speech, so as they are shut down, the brain struggles to cope with the demands of lengthy conversation; hence to the observer they reply with grunts or single word answers.

At the same time, the need for sleep returns to a similar level as the brain required the last time it went through this process, during the first two to three years of its life. *Melatonin*, the hormone released in our brain to trigger the sleep cycle, is released up to two hours later in the day. This has an impact on the sleep cycle, as the second part of our sleep, the REM or Rapid Eye Movement stage, which is normally from about 2am to 6am, is longer and later in the morning and frequently interrupted by the need to get up for school or college. Alcohol misuse during this time is shown to interrupt the vital development of the adult brain.

## After Adolescence

As the frontal regions of the brain are reconnected, the brain experiences a sudden rush of new thinking abilities. As the freshly exposed neural pathways are used, the brain further strengthens and speeds up the connections through further *myelination*. A learning or educational growth spurt often happens at this time. Sleep patterns return to their normal routines and personality is restored, often with a new set of individual beliefs. The brain continues to learn how to use its new abilities during the latter teenage years and into the twenties.

This is the stage when values and belief systems develop that are independent of their parents and teachers. New ideas and standards are set in the emerging adult brain and the teenager will often reassess the future they seek as adults.

# Social And Emotional Development

Throughout this chapter it is worth noting that all ages are approximate; as anyone who has had more than one child will know, each child grows differently through the stages. For example, some babies move from the first stage to the second at about 12-14 months, others at 16-18 months. Often children who move on earlier struggle, as the other children in their age group are not socially at the same stage. An example is when one toddler tries to play with other children as they have moved onto that social development stage, whilst the others all want to engage in solitary play.

## Self-identity

The foundation for all humans is their own sense of identity and security in what they like. This is a fundamental state of being that is vital to their own personal success and growth and it is something learnt as infants.

During pregnancy, a baby's systems were regulated by those of their mother: they had the same vitamins she did, they experienced the same hormones that she did and this resulted in them co-regulating with her. This continues during infancy as an infant feeds or plays face-to-face games with their mother, experiences 'tummy time' and experiences care giving when they are distressed. This is why the parental figures have such highly attuned sensitivity to the emotions of the baby, as they are in effect taking responsibility for helping to manage them. The holding, rocking, soothing, feeding and changing when a baby is distressed help the infant's brain to connect the right neurons for coping with emotional overload. They are in effect teaching the *amygdala* what it feels like to be content and secure.

This bonding process is the beginning of the development of 'I' and can be affected by thousands of factors, such as birth trauma, post-natal depression, illness, disability, housing, education, support from professionals and so on. Many parents become concerned or guilty when they learn the impact of external (and internal) factors on the brain development of a baby, however this is where the concept of

## Social And Emotional Development

'good enough caregiving' is introduced. This is the theory that for a child it is not about the individual factors, but the overall impact that determines the impact of difficulties the child experiences - if the care is 'good enough' then professionals would expect the child to be develop normally and have resilience to challenges.

The scientific theory behind the bonding process between an infant and their parents says that if a child experiences enough protective factors then they can overcome the parts that are missed as a result of the other factors. Broadly speaking, if the influence of the protective factors outweighs the impact of the negative factors (or risks) then the infant will have the support it needs for healthy bonding and development. Even if, for whatever reason, this is not the case, it is possible to revisit this process, or overcome related difficulties, at later stages.

As a baby learns to rely on these experiences and have its needs met, it begins to understand that it has needs that will be met, and trust and security develop. This is the precursor for what will later become the 'sense of I', which is a fundamental part of every human: that they value themselves as people and that they value that their needs deserve to be met. When they are older and they feel threatened, overwhelmed, exhausted or stressed they will revisit their 'sense of I' to re-establish themselves. It may be that they watch a favourite TV programme, have a soapy bath, wear particular clothing, do a physical activity, meditate, eat a favourite meal or listen to their favourite music; there will be something that they do that allows them to securely access the *amygdala* and relates to the caregiving they experienced as infants when they were overwhelmed. In effect whenever they feel overwhelmed or threatened, they reset themselves by mobilising the *amygdala* to help them. If they don't reassure the amygdala it becomes overloaded with anxiety and stress and they find themselves struggling to cope until they do (this is what happens when people keep going until they become ill or experience burnout).

## Sex, alcohol and drugs

There are false ways of fooling ourselves into feeling as if we have reassured our 'sense of I'; these normally involve sex, drugs or alcohol.

Fear is closely linked to sexual arousal; theories suggest that when we are young we become familiar with our parents' voice pitch, but that when they are then conversing with someone else, we experience fear. This causes our *amygdala* to experience fear and safety feelings at the same time and it is suggested that this then links with our later sexual attractions. Therefore, when we feel threatened or are overwhelmed later on, we experience fear and we have been pre-conditioned that one way of dealing with that is through the safety of a loved one, or a sexual mate. This can be seen through sex games, such as doctor and patient, teacher and student, and can be seen through sexual positions. Unfortunately, this can also lead to predatory sexual behaviours or risky sexual behaviours as the individual attempts to feel the safety and security of sexual pleasure.

Drugs and alcohol often give us the feeling of wellbeing, enjoyment or pleasure normally associated with us revisiting our 'sense of I' in the *amygdala*. Different drugs have different effects on various parts of the brain, but normally they are initially consumed for the experience they give the user. Both drug use and alcohol can then lead to a vicious cycle. For the period that the individual is using them, they experience the pleasurable effects of the drug (I am including alcohol as a drug at this point). However, once they come down or sober up, the original pain is still there (often made worse by the side effects of the drug). Therefore, they reuse the drug as that made them feel all right and so the cycle begins. As they are not safely re-accessing their 'sense of I' then this cycle can continue for some time.

The security the infant feels allows it to appreciate its needs will be met and that it is safe to bond with the adults around them. And so begins the social and emotional journey. Very quickly, an infant learns to look at the moving shapes, it learns to focus and eventually make eye contact with its parents. The reactions they get from their parents when they pull a 'smile' mean that they get a rush of *endorphins* in their brain. For the baby this links smiling and laughter with a feel good factor and they learn to smile. The fact that they are soothed when they are angry or frustrated means they learn how to set their maximum temperature; they start to learn how to calm themselves down. Adults interacting with them entertain and teach them that they are important; they will learn to recognise their name. They learn to engage in games as they experience more *endorphin* rushes as the parents react to them playing the games; eventually this extends, until by the age of one or two they can self-sustain their interest in a toy or game without an adult being involved. Babies begin to relate different games and experiences to different people; they recognise the games they can do with their maternal figure and the different games that are played with their paternal figure. Eventually, this develops into them using body language, gestures and simple sounds to request a particular game from someone; however, at first they do not recognise that strangers do not know these games and so will become frustrated.

### Threats to self or gaps in social and emotional development

Very often older children (and many adults) who are feeling stressed, anxious or insecure about their 'sense of I' will revert to this stage of self-occupying or being 'self-centred' as others may see it. Once the cause of the insecurity or threat to their self-identity is over, they are then observed to return to their normal selves.

Sometimes we see older children, including teenagers, stuck at this developmental stage. Although they may wish to have a wider social life, their anxiety, low self-esteem, insecurity or self-consciousness

## Social And Emotional Development

holds them back. This is often due to gaps in their social and emotional development that cause a lack of trust in the 'sense of I'. This can be overcome by identification of the gaps and helping the child to overcome these. One way of identifying if this is the case, and what the gaps are, is The Curtis Scale. This can be downloaded free from www.thekidcalmer.com/curtis.

As a baby feels more secure about their parents and themselves, they will cope with being with other people for longer periods of time. They will use different noises to signify meaning and the early formation of words occurs. Unfortunately, for those infants whose needs were not met at birth, they will have quickly learnt that they are wasting their time crying and attempting to engage with others, so they are less likely to want to speak or indeed may have become mute.

Babies at this stage want other people in their world to entertain them. As they begin to crawl or walk, it is to get something for themselves or to take something to someone to engage with them, for example taking a toy to an adult so the adult plays with the toy with the child. If there are other children or babies around, then it is likely at this stage that they will see them as insignificant or as a threat; hence they can be seen hitting each other in a bid to fend them off and get the attention back. Their concentration extends, they are able to self-sustain their play for longer periods of time. At this age babies are unlikely to recognise 'no' as a boundary, however they will recognise their parents' tone of voice and eventually relate it to whatever they were trying to do.

## Recognising The Rights Of Others

As a baby grows, generally between 12 and 18 months, they start to recognise there are other children. Initially they play alongside them, not interested in the other child, but eventually they start to watch them, sometimes for great periods of time. As they listen to stories, the child will begin to recreate favourite parts or choose particular stories.

The toddler has spent their life so far finding ways to get self-satisfaction and entertainment from the world around them; it has always been about them up until this stage. This has helped them to develop a sense of self-security; confidence in knowing their needs will be met and the adults look after them. They become interested in what another child is doing, they wander over to them and interfere, often barging, pushing or snatching. Initially this is an attempt to get the other child to entertain them, however this progresses to a desire to have the toys that the other child has and eventually becomes a way of initiating contact. This frequently is achieved by using their bodies, by pushing or punching the other child, maybe snatching their toy, in a bid to get that interaction.

**The impact of technology on social and emotional development**

One of the big things the 21$^{st}$ century has brought is an avalanche of technology. Whilst, when we were younger, there may have been one computer per house, now it is usual to have a laptop each, a phone and maybe a tablet.

The availability of technology for children has increased too; it is possible to get gadgets for infants upwards. However, it is very likely that this could affect a child's social and emotional development.

Socially, most technology for young children is based on the individual. So rather than learning about self-occupation in games, and the social skills of taking turns and sharing, children are being engaged by the technology. In this case, rather than developing their independence, the technology could be seen as acting as a surrogate parent interacting with them. It may be a game on a tablet, it may be television, and the important thing to recognise is that when used often, it is unhealthy. A fundamental part of the 'sense of I' is that a child is comfortable with being with themselves and occupying themselves. This is a stepping-stone used to develop their ability to play with other children and extend their own games into a cooperative game. As a teen and later as an adult, there are many times when they will require the ability to self-occupy without the television; it may even be that they need to motivate themselves to complete a project or assignment.

If someone has spent their early years relying on technology to entertain them, then they are likely to have developed fewer intrinsic motivation skills to be able to entertain themselves or fuel them to

## Social And Emotional Development

complete work, assignments, projects, revision and so on. Socially, the impact could then mean that they are then reliant on others or technology to help them interact with others. Rather than seek to establish friendships, the risk is that they make friends and interact in a bid to be entertained as they are unable to entertain themselves; in effect, they have become needy.

There is an important emotional significance here too; using excessive technology at a young age could interrupt the vital process of learning to cope with emotions. Infants and toddlers learn how to calm down from extreme emotions by the regulation given by parents: they soothe, they reassure, they meet needs, and they teach a child how to do things. The reason these emotions are experienced is often to do with play or basic needs. Regularly using technology to entertain or pacify a bored child reduces the frequency of them experiencing these emotions and, more importantly, them having their emotions externally regulated by a parent. A parent externally regulating a child's emotions connects the neural pathways for the children to learn to do this themselves. It is part of the process of learning to self-regulate their emotions. By consistently being pacified by technology, the neural pathways will not be accessed as much and so the risk is that the child becomes dependent on being externally regulated. Dummies are example of how children can become reliant on external support to calm them - there are parents who spend many hours hunting for the lost pacifier, as that is the only thing that will calm their child.

Finally, there are another important emotional hormones at play here too – the *dopamine* and *opioid* systems. *Dopamine* is the pleasure-seeking drug; generally, it is good for us and helps us to keep going to achieve a goal. When we achieve that goal, the hormone *opioid* system gives us a pleasure rush, which makes us feel good and counteracts the *dopamine*. Technology will often give us positive rushes in quick succession to engage us (for example achievements in games) and so it teaches us from a young age to expect immediate rewards. Even messaging apps on phone nowadays tell you when it has been delivered, read and if the recipient is replying. This all leads the brain to expect immediate rewards for everything, they want it now and do not want to have to wait for the reward or treat at the end of the day/week.

Technology is amazing, but it is important to bear in mind that healthy tech. habits should start before gadget use becomes an issue.

By now, a toddler has a grasp of the basic emotions, such as fear, joy, disgust, surprise, sadness, interest, or anger; they are able to accept basic limitations put on them by their parents. As their brain does a massive job of wiring up their experiences into fresh areas of the brain, they desire more independence from their parents, but then find themselves out of their depth very quickly. This results in their

## Social And Emotional Development

brain becoming confused and resulting in mood swings and tantrums as the developing frontal lobes become overloaded. These tantrums are a result of emotional overwhelm and require a similar amount of care and soothing as when they were overwhelmed as infants. By doing this consistently a toddler learns where the boundary is, that no means no, and how to handle the emotions that go alongside that. In terms of social and emotional development in the brain, this is a vital stage as a child is learning how to cope with not getting what they want. Negotiation and trying to converse with a child going through a tantrum rarely works, as at this age their vocabulary is so limited they cannot express the overwhelm and do not have the skills to understand the choices. Tantrums in a three- or four-year-old are slightly different; they originate from the same cause, overload in the frontal lobes, however as a child has a higher level of cognition by this stage they can be more aware of the advantages of having a tantrum, especially if it means they get their own way.

A toddler at this stage can express their own basic needs, like thirst or hunger, although the ability to recognise they need the toilet is often still developing. Over time, they develop more self-aware emotions, like pride, shame or guilt. They start to learn social etiquette, such as saying please and thank you, and will join in with a game with another child supervised by an adult. For the parents there is often repetitive enforcement of social skills, such as saying please, thank you, not snatching and taking turns - requiring high levels of adult involvement in the initial stages of socially interacting with other children. After the initial bumpy starts this develops into an ability to talk to other children, the young child learning to take turns in speaking and listening in addition to needing to take turns in their play.

By the time they are three or four, a child is able to interact and take turns in simple games with other children. Often this is dependent on some known rules, for example, they can play 'mummies and daddies' together as there is a clearly defined set of shared rules, and begin to be able to share; they develop friendship skills and have one or two close friends. They understand the impact of their behaviour on others - they have recognised the rights of other children.

## Interacting With Others

As a child becomes familiar with the social conventions of friendship, they learn to form longer lasting relationships with other children. They are able to give and take; they can make simple requests independently. They share with other children, with very few interventions needed from adults. Independent play develops more of a familiar sequence and they negotiate with other children to extend the game.

Role-play (whether dressing up or small world) recreates situations they are familiar with (such as school) or things they have seen (such as their favourite movie). Each time there is probably a conversation about the allocation of parts, which over time develops into a negotiation. This is an important milestone dependent on the 'sense of I', as it's only with a secure sense of their own identity and self-value that they are able to stand up for themselves and justify why they should be so-and-so.

Parents begin to see the formation of independent personality around the age of four or five. They have a developing sense of trust and can recognise the adults they trust, they listen with interest to people talking about something, which interests them, and they have a positive view of their own qualities. During this time, children also learn to adapt their speech for the listener – the way they speak to an adult is different to how they speak to a toddler.

The child feels success as they start to follow rules without need for constant praise and reward. Some external motivation is still required until they are seven or eight, and many would argue that this continues into adulthood. As their understanding of the rules develops, the child develop a moral code and often become the 'policeman' or the 'policewoman', where they become obsessed about rule following and happily tell tales on those that do not. It is only later that they learn rules are not black and white and that some are flexible.

As a child learns the need for rules, they become more socially competent in their behaviour. By this stage, they are only having infrequent tantrums, if any at all. Their brain has learnt how to deal with emotional overload and deploys a number of coping mechanisms and distraction techniques to ensure the frontal lobes do not become overwhelmed. Provided their 'sense of I' is secure, then this happens independently without much notice. The child is able to understand the consequence of their actions; they will be able to recognise how it affects others and will use this to constrain their behaviour within acceptable limits.

## Recognising The Needs Of Others

By now, a child is seven or eight and they are developing the multiple voices that make up their conscience. For some children, this is a frightening time, as they complain about hearing voices inside their head; over time, their parents reassure them that this is good and will help them to make decisions. Eventually, this is recognised as the conscience, using the value and belief systems of their parents and teachers. Although never truly free of the need for external motivation, most behaviour compliance by this stage is internally motivated.

Socially a child is becoming a true friend, they make complex decisions and take actions to improve the lives of others, have an advanced concept of fairness and know how to be a good friend; in turn this leads to a closer bond with a small circle of peers. Their play becomes more complex as they make up new rules for games or extend their play to fantasy or imaginary play that they have not experienced or seen. Collaborative play is learnt; this involves understanding the 'rule system' for this particular game at this particular time (for example, understanding a friend's house rules for Monopoly), or combining existing games to make a new game (for example joining Star Wars role play with Toy Story). Different perspectives begin to be understood, an important skill for some games like football for example, where it is vital that they are able to understand a teammate's intentions to move to a particular space and not just pass the ball directly to them.

In friendship circles, a child emerges as an empathetic friend, taking steps to understand the motivations and emotions of others; trying to independently resolve disputes within the friendship group. Parents turn from enforcers of social rules to advisers for their child as they help teach them how to resolve friendship problems. A child's personality develops and they are able to express opinion about things in their lives and make decisions about what they would like to do.

# Reforming Sense Of Identity

During the teenage years as the brain rewires itself, the child learns to reform their 'sense of I'. Pre-pubescent children will often have developed sociable personalities interested in learning about their hobbies and things that interest them. Their brain is craving new experiences and learning to utilise the millions of new neurons that have grown. Socially they are in a period of change, they move to schools where they need to take responsibility for organising themselves and following new routines. Their friendship group changes as the child makes decisions about who will be in their circle of friends. This is also the stage where they are likely to become curious about romantic relationships; even if they do not form any, there is likely to be much social conversation about them.

However, as puberty hits, the teenager's brain goes into a more animalistic state. The frontal lobes are used far less and so the brain relies on the mammalian emotional brain to respond. Physically their head drops, they find eye contact difficult, conversation is limited to minimal responses; all skills that the brain relies on for a good 'sense of I', the brain is making feel insecure. As demands, basic or complex, are placed on the child they react with extreme emotions, as their brain misses the guiding hand of the frontal lobes to cope with expectations. For a parent, this stage is similar to the learning they had to do with their toddler child; in essence, the same process is happening again in the brain. The teen will want to isolate themselves for long periods of time and it is important in families that expectations around family mealtimes and days out are maintained in order to help their brain retain social functions.

Socially, the teenage mind feels insecure, so will want to fit in with a group to make it feel safe. This can lead to situations where groups form, with no real guiding inhibitors to stop inappropriate or sometimes vicious comments or actions. The individual teen mind can be very unkind to others and the teenage group mind amplifies this. The emotional brain is desperate to have a sense of identity and belonging to make it feel secure, making the teen very susceptible to being easily influenced in a number of ways. Any problems within the friendship group are met with very dramatic reactions and a parent often needs to act as an adviser and mediator to help their teen's emotional brain relearn how to respond to the situation.

At the same time as the voice of reason that tells their mind something is too risky or dangerous disappears, they are faced with a number of opportunities to experiment with drugs, drinks, sex and even weapons. Each of which can give a false sense of security in the mammalian brain. In a bid to feel safe against perceived threats, for example, a teenage member of a gang may be encouraged to carry a knife or a (sometimes real) gun. Romantically, this is a stage where the increased levels of hormone mean that early sexual experimentation is on the teenage mind, with the female mammalian

## Social And Emotional Development

brain often focussing on making themselves more attractive for potential mates, and the male mammalian brain more likely to seek to prove themselves with early sexual conquests.

As a teenager emerges from puberty, they experience an intellectual growth spurt as the brain cells are reconnected. The older teen develops their own set of values and beliefs, sometimes in conflict with those of their parents. As they re-establish their 'sense of I' new things become important to them and their personality develops into that of a young adult. Developmentally this is the time when they start to learn about independent living and take responsibility for the course of their lives.

# Having Difficult Conversations

Throughout this book, there will be references to the need to have a conversation with your child about the possible threats they could encounter. It is a sad fact of the modern world that even staying in their bedrooms your child will be facing threats that you as a parent cannot control. Therefore, it is often far better to have preventative conversations so that your child is equipped to know what to do, rather than panic and try to hide it from you when it does happen.

Completely isolating a young person from technology altogether brings in other difficulties, as the moment they then have to use the technology that they are bound to encounter, they will not have the skills to cope with it.

The content of the conversations will vary depending on the threat, your situation and your child (their age, ability, comprehension).

There are two types of conversation as a modern parent you may need to use, information giving and problem solving. Information giving situations are when you need to educate your child about something, be it sex, pornography, grooming, viruses to name but a few. Problem solving conversations are times when your child needs your ear and guidance. By having established a sense of security and trust in the first type of conversation, you are more likely to have proven to your child that you are a non-judgemental ally that they need when they encounter difficulties and need to turn to someone.

## Information Giving Conversations

Although you are giving information to your child, this needs to be a conversation. The stages of the conversation are broken down into steps to help you to have as much structure as you need. As you talk, listen to the questions your child is asking; apart from answering them you will be able to reassure them before you leave the conversation.

The final step is the most critical: you want to reassure your child they will not have done anything wrong if they come to you with a problem, whether it is with their friends or with technology. As they grow, it becomes increasingly important that you are an ally of theirs during their teenage years, rather than a dictator.

You may find sometimes you need to revisit this conversation depending on your child and you will notice the conversation is simpler for younger children who have not developed their conscience (normally around the age of eight).

For under eights:

- When they could come across the threat;
- What they'll experience/see/notice/hear;
- What they should do about it;
- Reassurance and security.

For older children:

- Ensure your child is ready to listen;
- When they could come across it;
- What they'll experience/see/notice/hear;
- What they should do about it;
- How does that make them feel?
- What questions do they have?
- Reassurance and security.

## Problem Solving Conversations

As parents, you spend the first few years setting the boundaries for your child, what they can and cannot do, where the line is. They respect your view and see the world as a very black and white place where your word is the limit.

However, as they develop their conscience at around the age of eight, they start to get their own views and can become 'mini-adults' in many respects. During adolescence, their brain is busy rewiring and very often, this sense of personal identity is once again lost, before re-emerging at around the age of 15-17.

During this time, the role of a parent changes from the enforcer of rules to the ally for the child. You position yourself in such a way that your child will come to you for help with their difficulties, rather than turning away from you. To help you with this process, you can use a four-step conversation.

The four steps:

- Safety,
- Silence,
- Talking,
- Support.

**Safety**

Initially you want your child to not perceive you or the conversation as a threat. Maybe you are going to be doing something together, playing a game, walking the dog, cooking. This helps to make sure that the conversation is not a face-to-face one. Face-to-face conversations are the hardest to have as instantly you psychologically take opposite sides, whereas if you are both looking at something together then the conversation takes a different tone.

**Silence**

When helping someone to resolve an issue, or even deal with loss or grief, an important early step is to give him or her the space to allow their head to sort the thoughts out. Crowding an overwhelmed brain by asking lots of questions, like 'how do you feel?', just causes more overload and often causes a defensive response. However, sitting with someone in silence makes it all right to sort those thoughts out, to fit them into the existing schema in our brains and to slot them into the various compartments of our experience.

**Talking**

As humans, we are constantly trying to help other people by suggesting what they could do or say; with children, many parents find they even finish their sentences in a bid to be helpful. When faced with an issue, this is not helpful; let the silence grow and as it does and they work out their thoughts, you will find you move to the third step, when your child asks questions or verbalises their thoughts. For you, this stage is predominantly listening, with the use of questions for clarifications or for refocus.

**Support**

It is only now that you can offer support and advice, after your child's brain has off-loaded their worries and concerns. For many they will be feeling better; you listening will have helped them reflect on their problem and process the emotions. For others they will need to hear what you would do or even about the time you faced a similar situation. You will need to reassure them and offer guidance, whilst not imposing your will on what is already a complex problem for your child.

# Part Two – The Parent's Guide to the Modern World

# Social Lives, Community And The Wider World

Humans are social animals, we like to have contact with others, and we develop as a race through collaboration and cooperation. The modern world is very different to the society you and I grew up in, and so naturally, the way we socialise has changed. Much socialising by children outside of school is done via technology and they are very likely to be chatting or messaging whilst playing games. This changes the way that we parent our children and what we need to watch out for.

## Peer Pressure

Part of growing up and finding their own identity is a vital part of children's development, particularly during the teenage years. During the teenage years, the brain is rewiring and in many respects reverts to the level of a toddler. In middle adolescence, a teenager brain starts to connect the new parts of the frontal lobes and this allows them to reconnect with their own personality. This in turn helps them to develop their own personality, belief systems and sense of what is right or wrong.

As they struggle to connect with themselves and their friendship groups, children will often become judgemental or unkind to others in a bid to make themselves feel better or be part of a group. The power of the psychology of a group can often result in the same victim being targeted by members of a social circle; with the members of the group wanting to be 'in' with the group, this increases the need to be 'seen' to be doing what the group wants.

Group minds are created when a few individuals form together to create a social circle of some kind and the members of the group will put aside their own needs for the needs of the group at certain times. At its most basic this can be a relationship, where both people put aside some of their views or beliefs in order to empower the relationship. At its most extreme, we see riots, where a large group of people combine against a 'common enemy', such as the government or police. In the latter group, particularly we often see individuals risking their own personal safety or beliefs for the common cause. Supporters of sports teams are another example of how group minds work, where one group unites to demean or put down the opposing team through their chants, although on an individual basis many tone down this behaviour and taunt a friend who supports a different team. The human race, like many animals, is driven to be part of a group.

A very simple demonstration of this is a person's social circle. Imagine the scene: a group have not met up for some time and arrange to meet up for a meal. Now one of the party does not really like the restaurant, but all of the others are really keen, so they agree to go, they do what is best for the group. Whilst there they enjoy talking to their friends, they realise it has like they have never been apart and they had forgotten how much they loved being with them, how they made them feel. They are careful to make sure they pick something from the menu they enjoy, but it is never quite, how they like it, they did not really want to come to this restaurant after all. Nevertheless, they eat it and pay at the end, because they are enjoying the group experience. One of the friends suggests they go on somewhere after. Now they know that they have to be up early and they have a million reasons why they need to go home, however they suggest to the group that they all go 'for a quick one'. Several hours later they love it, they feel like they have not done this in ages and time passes quickly. Humans all forfeit little things to be part of a group, we all feel peer pressure at different times.

## What are the risks?

For those teenagers who are feeling low or insecure, this has a huge impact. Their brain is already struggling with reduced reasoning and self-control skills because of the rewiring process. They are often desperate to be part of a social circle or group. So very often, they have two routes to follow: they either isolate themselves and reject the group, or they submit to whatever peer pressure is put on them to be part of the group.

Rejection from a group can increase the isolation and depression for a child. Many teens choose to avoid this by forfeiting their beliefs to the needs and desires of the group. This combined with the changes in their brain cause a risk-taking type of behaviour where teenagers can seem not to be bothered about the impact of their actions. This can result in bullying, offending or self-injurious behaviour, such as drug or alcohol use.

When will this pressure stop?!

## Peer Pressure

**Dos**

Do activities and ensure your child gets different experiences to help use the different areas of the brain. This will then help them to develop their own personality, likes and dislikes.

Be alert to the peer pressure your child is under.

Be the friendly, non-judgemental ear for your child. They will encounter sex, drugs, alcohol, porn, and bullying whether you like it or not – it is far better for them to have you to turn to when they do.

**Don'ts**

Compare the pressure your child is under to what you experienced; today's world is very different.

Deny your child the emotions they are feeling as they experience social problems, your child is unlikely to have learnt that they will fade and they will feel very real to them.

# Gangs

Humans like to be part of groups, they like to belong and relate to other people. This relates back to tribal days, when it was safer to be part of a tribe than to be individual. Tribe members protected each other, hunted together, shared food and so on.

In the modern world, this underlying need is still present. In work places people form small tribes, whether they are team or social groups. Many millions are part of tribe followings, such as sports teams or fan clubs. In addition, whilst many of these do not have the same function as the prehistoric tribes, they do share the concept of the group mind.

Every group has a collective need; it may be one of five functions:

- Survival or meeting basic needs, such as victim support groups or tenants' associations. These groups are about collaborative survival.
- Beating other groups or to achieve success together, such as sports fans. These groups want to be the best or win competitions, showing their prowess.
- Destructive groups, for example pressure groups. These groups seek to destroy a policy, an individual, another group or even some of its own members if the external primate 'kill' is not achieved.

- Empowering or developing the individuals, such as business growth networks or sports teams. These groups seek to train, skill up, challenge or otherwise improve the individual performance of its members.
- Entertainment groups, for example fan clubs or fashion houses, are about group members having a shared interest in something and wanting to display their membership.

Gangs tend to fall into the second function, although the individuals in the group may have joined for perceived basic survival needs (for example a threat) or the group can become a destructive group and either be trying to destroy a rival gang or a weakling or traitor in their group. Gangs can be common in areas where there are high levels of poverty, distrust or social exclusion and commonly feature some form of criminality or delinquent behaviour.

**What are the risks?**

Once someone starts to become involved in a gang, it can be very hard to leave. This is particularly due to the concept of the group mind. The group mind is collective and the individuals in the group will all concede individual needs for the sake of the group. An example of this is the number of people who are quite meek or mild, who become screaming fans at a ball game. At its most extreme very ordinary law abiding citizens get caught up in the group mind of a riot; at these times they concede to the destructive aims of the group mind and join in with the vandalism or looting. The same can be seen in children being caught up in gangs.

This is particularly true when a child feels a low 'sense of I', for example when they are going through puberty and their brain is restricted many teens suffer with low self-esteem and struggle with their own identity. If they feel anger or resentment against their parents or society, then they may join to go against society or to prove a point. They could even feel abandoned or alone in this world and want to feel part of something. If this is the case, it is very easy to then be caught up in the powerful attraction of the gang with a very established identity.

Individual children may want to overcome hardship, poverty or other barriers by showing the world how powerful they can be; they want to impress people. Gangs accommodate them very easily as this is consistent with making the group mind more powerful. Internally this can then lead to the 'alpha male'

syndrome, where two or three males or females seek to become the most powerful and influential in the group.

| Dos | Don'ts |
|---|---|
| Always remember the power of a strong 'sense of I'. | Ban them from being with a gang. |
| Help your child to join other groups. | Be judgemental, it will only make them move further away from you. |
| Understand your child (particularly during puberty) will feel safer in groups. | |
| Be open to listening about your child's experiences. | |

## Knives And Weapons

There are a number of reasons that children or teenagers may carry weapons. These predominantly come down to some kind of insecurity or threat to their 'sense of I'. Let us look at the reasons more closely:

- Defence – I am worried someone wants to hurt me.
- Intimidation – I am not getting my own way; I want to scare others.
- Belonging – I have to do this to fit in with a group, I want to impress, and I am not secure with my belonging without it.

**Knives**

A knife is a very personal weapon; it is there for people who will be close to us, people who we intend to let close to us. This implies that if someone is carrying it for self-defence then they expect the person threatening them to be within very close proximity. The facts that the threat can get so close to them makes them feel insecure, highlighting the need for some form of defence. Moreover, unlike other weapons, such as a gun or something to hit people with, a knife does not require a great deal of space to use. If a child is anxious, then they are going to be responding with adrenaline and a fear response, making them feel more threatened and increasing the likelihood of them using the knife to 'defend' themselves.

If a knife were being carried to intimidate someone, it would need to be someone who they know they can get close to. On these occasions, it is far more likely that it will be used as a sign of power, rather than a weapon. They will want others to see that they have it and will draw it to show it off or to make people back off.

Another reason for carrying a knife may be a badge of honour within a gang, where unlike a gun (fake or real) it is to be seen up close. Guns, chains, iron bars, machetes and other larger weapons are about being seen at a distance, not so with a knife. If they want to show other gang members that you are 'tooled up', then a knife can be a discreet weapon to carry that won't be obviously spotted and will only need to be used when an attacker has got through the gang's 'outer defences'.

**Guns**

Guns are a very different story; they portray power and are meant to intimidate others. Carrying a gun implies a subliminal message that a person will not accept being messed with. Shooting someone can be indiscriminate too; the power of making instant life or death decisions about other people's lives may mirror the power emotions they felt

## Knives And Weapons

when playing computer games, or allow the power to compensate for the pain they have felt about other situations.

If they are to be used for defence, then it will normally be for a target further away than arm's length. In these cases, it may be that the person feels powerless and so does not want to risk people getting close to them as they may overpower them.

A teen carrying a gun in order to fit in with a gang is doing so in order to impress other gang members or promote their social standing within the group. They are using it as a badge of honour to show that they are powerful, fearless or equal to others who carry guns.

# Machetes, pipes, chains, sticks, clubs and other weapons

It's in case any of the children attack me

These tend to be more improvised and relate to more immediate threats. In the case of these being used for defence, they tend to be makeshift. In the cases where these weapons have been planned, they will be easily accessible in areas where they are expecting trouble; these generally are used for intimidation first and defence second. Finally, it is important to consider that someone publicly carrying something, like a machete, in order to fit in with a gang has little regard for the consequences; by carrying a weapon that cannot be hidden, they are risking being caught by police; in effect their insecurity is putting them in danger.

### What are the risks?

It only takes one flash of emotion to move from a weapon carrier to a killer. Whilst a teen may want to feel safe or powerful by carrying a

## Machetes, pipes, chains, sticks, clubs and other weapons

weapon, as we have discussed it is only a sign of insecurity. This, in itself, implies that they may not be able to cope with their emotions and so could be at risk of 'lashing out' with the weapon, just as others make a barbed or hurtful comment and then feel immediate guilt. Unfortunately, the latter can be solved with an apology; the former can have fateful consequences for others and for their liberty.

| Dos | Don'ts |
|---|---|
| Make your child feel secure about their 'sense of I'. | Let them idolise people who carry weapons, in real life or films. |
| Be open about why people carry weapons if they pay any interest to them. | If your child does end up with a weapon, do not scare and punish them and make them feel more insecure; instead understand, empathise, build trust and security within the family unit to begin with. |

# Drugs

**What drugs are out there?**

There are many forms of drugs out there that can be abused; here are the most common ones that you may come across to help you to identify them and their side effects.

| Drug | What it looks like | What the effects are | Long term effects |
|---|---|---|---|
| Alcohol | There are many different forms of alcohol, watch out for your teen being able to order it online using your password to shopping sites. | Decreased attention; Increased risk-taking behaviour; Increased risk of being involved in violent behaviour; Increased risk of suicidal acts; Emotional problems; More likely to have unprotected sex or be the victim or | Increased chance of adult alcohol abuse; Decreased memory; Decreased brain growth; Risk of: Heart disease; Stroke; Liver disease |

|  |  | perpetrator of a sexual assault. | or cancer; Mouth cancer; Pancreatitis. |
|---|---|---|---|
| Amphetamines (speed, whizz, base, billy) | Powder, tablets or liquid | Reduced diet; Difficulty sleeping; Long come down causing lethargy and difficulty concentrating. | Lowers immune system; Anxiety; Depression; Paranoia; Irritability and aggression; Vein damage if being injected. |
| Ayahuasca | A plant infused in tea (traditionally from South American plants, but variants can be made with plants in other | Hallucinations; Nausea; Vomiting; Sweating; Tremors. | Long term effects when mixed with anti-depressants. |

|  |  |  |  |
|---|---|---|---|
|  | countries) |  |  |
| Bath salts (not Epsom Salts used for bathing) | Crystals to be snorted, injected, ingested or smoked | Headaches; Nausea; Panic attacks; Hallucinations. | Paranoia; Delusions; Heart attack; Kidney failure; Liver failure. |
| Cannabis | Dried plant leaves | Anxiety; Paranoia; Panic; Light headed, sick and faint (a 'whitey'). | Difficulties learning; Poor concentration; Lack of motivation; Increased risk of psychotic illnesses; Fertility reduction; Increased heart rate and pressure; Smoking related risks. |

| | | | |
|---|---|---|---|
| Cocaine | White powder | Overdose can cause death; Increased pulse and blood pressure; Flu-like symptoms. | Damaged cartilage in nose; Depression; Anxiety; Panic attacks; Vein damage; Increased risk of mental health problems. |
| Cough/cold remedies | Tablet or solution | Suppression of breathing rate – increase risk of respiratory arrest; Nausea/vomiting; Constipation; Sweating; Itching; Mood swings; Lethargy. | Lower blood pressure; Kidney failure; Liver failure; Bleeding from the stomach. |
| Crack | Small white rocks | Overdose can cause death; | Breathing problems; |

## Drugs

| | | | Increased pulse and blood pressure; Flu-like symptoms. | Depression; Anxiety; Panic attacks; Vein damage; Increased risk of mental health problems. |
|---|---|---|---|---|
| DMT | | White crystalline powder, or impure as yellow, pink or orange powder or solids. | Hallucinations; Individual reactions leading to fear and possibly self-harm. | Flashbacks; Unpleasant emotional experiences lasting for days; Raised blood pressure. |
| Ecstasy | | Tablets (known for their different pictorial imprints) or white powder (also known as MDMA or crystal) | Anxiety; Paranoia; Panic attacks; Psychosis; Dilated pupils; Increased heart rate; Tightening of | Memory problems; Anxiety; Depression; Liver and kidney problems; Heart problems. |

75

|  |  | jaw muscles; Dehydration; Over-drinking (as ecstasy can stop the production of urine); Raised temperature. |  |
| --- | --- | --- | --- |
| GBL | Oily liquid or capsule (converts to GHB after entering the body) | Reduced inhibitions (and increased risk of sexual assault); Drowsiness; Risk of unconsciousness and death. | Could cause: Insomnia; Anxiety; Difficulty concentrating; Hallucinations. |
| GHB | Oily liquid or capsule | Reduced inhibitions (and increased risk of sexual assault); Drowsiness; Risk of unconsciousness and death. | Could cause: Insomnia; Anxiety; Difficulty concentrating; Hallucinations. |
| Hash | Black or | Anxiety; | Difficulties |

|  | | | |
|---|---|---|---|
|  | brown lump of the resin from cannabis | Paranoia; Panic; Light headed, sick and faint (a 'whitey'). | learning; Poor concentration; Lack of motivation; Increased risk of psychotic illnesses; Fertility reduction; Increased heart rate and pressure. |
| Heroin | White powder (pure), or cut beige to brown | Dizziness; Vomiting; Overdosing leading to death. | Vein or artery problems (if injected); Gangrene; Infections |
| Ketamine | Liquid or tablets/powder (street ketamine) | Can paralyse you for a period; Hallucinations; Easy to injure self and not feel | Bladder problems; Abdominal pain; Liver |

|  |  |  | |
|---|---|---|---|
|  |  | it. | damage. |
| Khat | Green plant | Suppresses appetite; Insomnia; Confusion. | High blood pressure; Heart problems; Inflame mouth; Tooth decay; Anxiety; Depression. |
| Kratom | Capsule or leaves for smoking or making tea | Nausea and vomiting; Sweating; Itching; Constipation; Delusions; Lethargy, including sudden sleepiness; Hallucinations; Reduced breathing; | Insomnia; Loss of weight; Darkening of skin; Cravings. |

|  |  | Tremors; Paranoia. |  |
| --- | --- | --- | --- |
| LSD | Squares of paper with pictures on them | Tired; Anxious; Depressed; Hallucinations. | Exacerbate underlying mental health conditions. |
| Magic mushrooms | Raw or dried to make tea | Tiredness; Nausea; Stomach pain; Diarrhoea. | Again a risk for those with mental health conditions. |
| Mandrax | Tablets in a range of colours, to be crushed and smoked in a pipe | Loss of muscle control; Headaches; Stomach cramps; Aggression. | Weight loss; Depression; Insomnia; Seizures. |
| Mephedrone | Fine white or yellow powder | Nausea; Paranoia; Anxiety; Hallucinations. | Reduced circulation; Insomnia; Loss of memory; Sweating. |

| | | | |
|---|---|---|---|
| Methamphetamine | Tablets, powder or crystals | Reduced appetite; Increased heart rate and blood pressure; Long come-down. | Psychosis; Brain damage. |
| Mescaline | Green button shaped seeds for drying or mixing with water | Hallucinations; Headaches; Vomiting; Anxiety; Panic. | |
| Nitrates/poppers | Liquid in small bottles | Nausea; Faintness; Headache; Low blood pressure; Unconsciousness; Burns the skin; Possible death if swallowed. | |
| PCP | Pill, tablet, crystal, liquid | Panic; | Difficulty breathing; |

# Drugs

| | | Paranoia; Aggression; Psychosis. | Vein damage (if injected); Memory problems; Poor appetite. |
|---|---|---|---|
| Psilocybin | Dried mushrooms, often put on food or mixed with food to hide taste | Tiredness; Nausea; Stomach pain; Diarrhoea; Hallucinations; Increased heart rate; Sweating followed by chills; Numbness of tongue or mouth. | Flashbacks, depression, panic, psychosis or delusions |
| Rohypnol | Tablets, capsules, suppositories | Short-term memory loss; Sleepiness. | Addiction can lead to withdrawal symptoms. |
| Salvia | A dried leaf for chewing or smoking | Hallucinations; Risk of | Throat and lung irritations. |

|  |  |  | psychosis. |
|---|---|---|---|
| Skunk | Strong variants of cannabis | Anxiety; Paranoia; Panic; Light headed, sick and faint (a 'whitey'). | Difficulties learning; Poor concentration; Lack of motivation; Increased risk of psychotic illnesses; Fertility reduction; Increased heart rate and pressure; Smoking related risks. |
| Solvents | Glues, gases, aerosols | Mood swings; Aggression; Hallucinations; Vomiting; Blackouts. | Muscle, lung, kidney damage. |
| Steroids | Tablets or liquids for | Paranoia; | Affect growth |

|   |   |   |   |
|---|---|---|---|
|  | injection | Aggression; Mood swings. | development; Difficulty sleeping; High blood pressure; For males – erection problems, breast development, loss of hair, acne; For females – extra facial hair, loss of hair, deeper voice, smaller breasts, enlarged clitoris, acne. |
| Tobacco | Cigarettes, cigars, pipes, dried leaf | Nausea; Dizziness; Cough. | Chest infections; Cancer; Heart disease; Lung disease. |

**Dos**

Be open, supportive and non-judgemental with your child, they are very likely to come across drugs during their adolescence, so it is far better that you know about it.

Seek help if you are concerned about your child.

**Don'ts**

Shy away from having conversations about drugs, even if you do not know about them, you have had the experience of being a teenager and the pressures that are put on you.

# Gender

**What is so different?**

There are a myriad of different gender possibilities a child could identify with nowadays. This may mean that as a child grows from childhood to adolescence they can encounter some very deep questions about their own identity.

Here is a brief list of the different gender identity options:

**Male**

**Female**

**Transgirl** – a transgender person who is born male but identifies herself as a girl.

**Transboy** – a transgender person who is born female but identifies as a boy.

**Gender fluid** – a person who has features of, or varies between features of multiple genders.

**Agender** – someone without gender.

**Androgynous** – someone with a combination of male and female traits.

**Bigender** – someone who identifies with two genders.

**Non-binary** – an umbrella phrase to cover someone who does not identify as wholly male or female.

**Demi-boy** – someone who, despite being born male, identifies as only partially male.

**Demi-girl** – as demi-boy but for those born as females.

**Genderqueer** – another name for non-binary.

**Gender non-conforming** – someone who does not conform to the gender norms.

**Tri-gender** – someone who identifies all of the time or varies between three genders.

**All genders** – as pangender.

**Pangender** – someone who identifies with all gender types.

**Omnigender** – as pangender.

**Intersex** – conditions that arise from external and internal genitalia being of different sex.

## What are the risks?

The challenge for parents in the 21st century is that many did not experience the same level of openness about gender identity when they were children. There will be different questions raised by your

# Gender

children as they go through adolescence than you will have thought of. It is also far more socially acceptable to openly display and discuss gender identity and differences.

If a child identifies with a different gender from their birth gender, then it is important that they feel able to explore these feelings in safety without feeling threatened or judged. For some parents, this forces them to face some of their own beliefs and values, whilst trying to help their child. It is therefore important that as a parent you are comfortable with these concepts.

## The Parent's Guide to the Modern World

| **Dos** | **Don'ts** |
|---|---|
| Be open to listening to your child as they explore their gender identity. | Dismiss any curiosity your teen may be showing about gender, they will be asking questions in a bid to try to formulate their self-identity. |
| Be open, do not judge, remember your values are not your child's values. | |
| Bear in mind that younger children from toddler up until pre-teen are likely to role-play different gender types as they become aware of them. | |

# Sexuality

## What is so different?

As with gender identity, society is a lot more open to the different sexual preferences in the 21$^{st}$ century. This combined with gender identity gives a never-ending list of possibilities, for example someone may identify themselves as transsexual, but still find themselves sexually attracted to the opposite gender of their birth gender, in effect a lesbian trans-lady or a gay trans-man.

Sexual preferences can include:

**Straight** – someone who is sexually attracted to the opposite sex.

**Gay** – someone who is sexually attracted to someone of the same sex.

**Lesbian** – a female attracted to other females.

**Homosexual** – someone sexually attracted to the same sex.

**Bisexual** – someone who is attracted to males and females.

**Asexual** – someone who is not sexually attracted to others or disinterested in sexual activity.

**Polysexual** – someone sexually attracted to more than one gender.

**Pansexual** – someone not limited to sexual choice, regardless of gender or gender identity.

Romantic orientations are also considered separate from sexuality:

**Heteroromantic** – someone romantically attracted to someone of a different sex, gender or gender identity.

**Homoromantic** – someone romantically attracted to someone of the same sex, gender or gender identity.

**Biromantic** – someone romantically attracted to people of two sexes, genders or gender identities.

**Panromantic** – someone romantically attracted to multiple sexes, genders or gender identities.

**Aromantic** – someone who is not attracted to any sex or gender.

### What are the risks?

Whilst there is a societal openness about sexuality, unfortunately at the time children are likely to be questioning their sexual preferences, it is also the time that a number of changes happen in the brain. As was described in the first part of this book, the adolescent brain shuts down the frontal lobe region. This is the part of the brain that gives people their personality, values and stops them from taking things too far.

As this coincides with exploration of sexuality, it is common for teens to experience bullying and unkind comments from others. This can dent the confidence of the emergent young person, especially if their sense of sexual self-identity is not secure.

Teens need to feel they can talk to someone at these times; it is far safer for that to be a parent. One of the ways that groomers get children to trust them is by being the person that a child can open up to, particularly picking on young people who feel isolated. This is also a time where young people explore their sexuality with other people and can find themselves in uncomfortable situations where they feel pressurised into doing or saying things, even sexting or sharing inappropriate photos.

| **Dos** | **Don'ts** |
|---|---|
| Share your teenage experiences with your teen, without giving them all of the gory details; help them to understand that you were teenage too. | Impose your sexual values or beliefs, the choices your child is making are very different from the ones you made. |
| Set boundaries for your young teen about visitors to the home, however remember it is far better that you know where your teen is. | Do not pry about your child's relationship, be the ear for them to turn to. |
| Use the difficult conversation format from Part One to help structure any discussions you need to have. | |
| Ensure that your teen knows that no means no. | |

# Terrorism

Terrorism is defined in the Oxford Dictionary as 'the unofficial or unauthorised use of violence and intimidation in the pursuit of political aims'.

Terrorist acts have played a major part in world events, increasingly so in more recent years. Where an attack in Africa may not have made everyday news around the world 20 years ago, nowadays people are experiencing it live across the television and Internet. Attacks like those in the USA, UK, France, Belgium, Pakistan, Iraq, Afghanistan or the Middle East (plus many others) have become mainstream and far-reaching. Terrorists even take to social media to launch PR campaigns or share videos justifying their acts or showing murders.

The purpose of these acts often comes down to an ideological or political belief. The perpetrators use these traumatic events to create terror amongst people, aiming to make the public feel insecure. They seek to get people to question their own belief systems in order to give way to the terrorist's.

## What are the risks?

With the rise of technology and the easy access to information almost immediately from across the world, terrorism is no longer restricted to a few geographical areas. A terrorist act is worldwide and has far-reaching consequences.

This means that much of the information about such acts, which parents could previously have protected their children from, is now readily accessible. The impact of this is that acts of terrorism may be spoken about in front of children, in the playground and at school. Seeing coverage on television or the Internet, or even hearing about these acts, can be scary for a child. Young children especially only have a concept of their immediate world around them, so to them the threat may feel very close and potentially make them anxious. Older children may be curious about the events, trying to conceptualise the acts in their developing sense of right and wrong; they may even play goodies and baddies against the terrorists. For teenagers it may spark an interest in the horrific nature of the act, potentially for the insecure teen this could become an interest or an obsession about deaths.

# Terrorism

| **Dos** | **Don'ts** |
|---|---|
| For young children as they ask about terrorism help them to understand that there are bad people in the world and that you do everything that you can to keep them safe. | It is impossible to block out the impact of terrorism on the modern world, it is far better to educate your child so they do not pay an unhealthy interest or become anxious. |

With older children, explain to them that there are people in the world who try to scare us, just the same as there are other children in the playground who also scare us. We avoid them and ignore them being unkind, as they show us fear, we show them that we are not listening to them and that we are happy with our friends.

Encourage teenagers to be interested in the reasons why people decide to take such extreme action. Teach them the different points of view

involved and that there are cases for all belief systems.

# Radicalisation

Radicalisation is the process by which someone develops extreme beliefs about a cause, possibly leading to acts of extreme violence. With the advent of the Internet, people are becoming more aware of radicalisation, with extreme acts appearing on screens daily. However, there have been notable examples in history, such as Charles Manson's cult, in addition to the more recent actions of al-Qaeda or the so-called Islamic State.

There is no single route to radicalisation; every person's route is unique. However, along the way there will have been several key milestones:

- Socialisation with a group who seem to offer friendship or companionship to someone who may have felt isolated.
- Changes in their beliefs and their social circles leading to behaviour changes and a possible increase in high-risk behaviour leading to criminal acts.
- An increased devotion or commitment to a religion, person or group.

Interestingly a 2013 report by RAND found that whilst the Internet created opportunities to become radicalised, that it helps facilitate the process of radicalisation and that the Internet acts as an 'echo chamber' (providing evidence of an existing 'inner belief'), it is not a cause in itself. There is also no link between radicalisation and poverty or mental health difficulties; people who are radicalised can come from all levels of society.

**What are the risks?**

Children can be easily influenced and will not be as cautious as adults will be to approaches. They may be befriended by an extremist who gets to know them and offers them the kinship they feel they are missing. A child, particularly a teenager, will feel that they have found a friend, a romance or a mentor who understands them and looks out for them. They may even suggest that parents or their existing friends cannot be trusted.

As the relationship develops then a child may well be attracted to suggestions of risky behaviour, especially if they are a teenager. Small offending behaviour may start; behaviour will change as they become radicalised. Eventually this can develop into law breaking and an affiliation towards more extreme acts, such as violence, in response to their beliefs.

## Dos

Teach your child to be wary of people they meet online trying to chat to them in private.

Watch out for changes in behaviour and beliefs, especially if they adopt extreme positions about things. Take notice if they stop talking about the conversations they are having or start hiding chat boxes or their phone when you come into the room.

Be open as a family in talking about the causes of the violence and terrorism we see in the world.

Use the difficult conversation model to address any concerns you have without making your child feel like you are judging them.

## Don'ts

Be cross or angry if they start to show any extreme views, this will just cause them to hide it.

Radicalisation

# Phones

Telephones have changed hugely over the last 20 years. Back then, there would be one phone line in every house and the parents closely monitored its use. They were often fixed phones connected to a socket on the wall by a wire and where it was located was where you had the conversation. As phone technology developed, then these eventually became cordless and families would have to hunt the house looking for the handset (that was often languishing uncharged in someone's bedroom).

For those who had siblings, they would often squabble about whose turn it was to use the phone or even queue to use it (although this was useful for learning the art of negotiation). When arranging to meet friends, children would phone up their parents 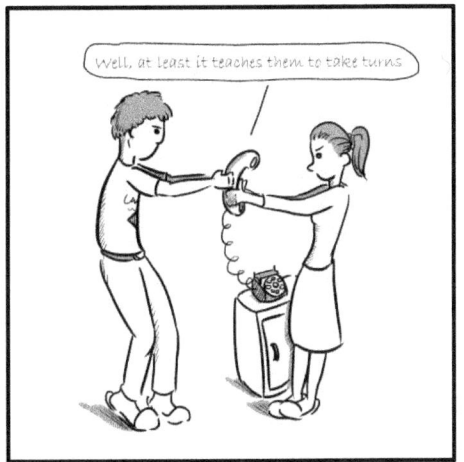 and ask to speak to them to arrange a time to meet up in a certain location. Public phone boxes contained books of everyone's phone numbers and you had to put in 10p before you could dial anyone. When travelling somewhere, parents would ask children to give them three rings to let them know they would arrived (this meant let the phone ring three times then hang up, as it did not cost anything).

Cell phones (as they were known in their early days) had been around for the affluent since the 1980s, but it was only in the late 1990s/early 2000s that these became accessible to everyday people. Initially all they did was make and receive calls, however the ability to send text messages revolutionised this. There were even television programmes devoted to the art of texting. These phones were often quite thick due to the large size of the batteries and it was common for people to wear them on their belts.

Nowadays it is rare for someone not to have a mobile phone and the society expectation is that people are available all of the time (even employers are providing mobiles so employees can be emailed late at night, with the expectation they have seen the message before the morning).

# Smartphones

Modern mobile phones are no longer just phones. They contain cameras, calculators, Internet access, games and far more. This combination of computer and telephone has coined the word smartphone. First used to describe a phone that could send emails and faxes in 1994, they became more readily available during the early 2000s and expanded massively with the launch of the iPhone from Apple in 2007.

The way people interact with smartphones is changing; voice recognition software can be used to control phones with inbuilt software or even through cars. In addition, watches and bracelets that project the phone's screen onto the wearer's arm have  also been launched. Currently these perform simple actions, however as this technology develops expect to see the smartphone's full capability be replicated.

## What are the risks?

Having seen mobile phones getting smaller for many years, there is a recent trend for their touch screens to be larger. This makes modern smart phones fragile, unlike many other children's toys. There is a large industry related to their fragility, such as insurance, screen protectors and cases to protect them from bumps and knocks. Some of the latest smartphones are waterproof for periods of time, however there is many a person who has dropped or sat on their phone and caused damage.

The very nature of smartphones makes it far harder for parents to monitor than it is for a computer, laptop or tablet. Pornography is easy to access and easier to stumble across. Savvy parents are downloading apps to block known pornography sites being accessed. Determined teenagers are learning how to bypass these, using different devices, setting up secret email addresses or using the power of the Internet to find out how to bypass them. Like it or not, parents need to teach their child what to do about pornography and how to choose to avoid it; blocking access to known sites will never stop a determined teen from being able to find it if they want to.

Even without pornography, there is a high risk that a child will be exposed to people seeking sex. A 2012 survey by the University of Southern California found that 17% of teenagers with smartphones were approached for sex online by someone they did not know. Instant messaging potentially allows people in a local area to contact a child just because they are on the same instant messaging system. Downloaded software, called apps, allowing users to connect for dating or just for sex, may rely on a simple tick box or confirmation that users are over the lower age limit.

The sharing of inappropriate photos contributes to the risks a teen faces. According to a 2008 survey by the National Campaign to Prevent Teen and Unplanned Pregnancy and CosmoGirl.com, 22% of all teen girls had shared or sent nude or semi-nude photos of themselves online. This included 11% of 13–16 year old girls! In the same survey, a third of teen boys and 25% of teen girls admitted that they had seen nude/semi-nude photos that were meant to be private. This highlights that children are not only sending inappropriate pictures of themselves, they are also sharing them. In addition, technology is making it easier for children to be able to take videos/pictures and send them (often through Instant Messaging systems), and others can easily forward, take a screen shot or just show other children the images.

Smartphones simplify purchases, via the Internet and through apps, by remembering and securely storing bank or card details. Purchases can often be made with only one or two clicks. This makes life very easy, particularly if you are after something in a hurry. However, this also makes it very easy for children to accidentally (or even purposely) purchase things. For example, parents may choose to install a parental control app on their child's phone, but to do that they had to purchase it from the phone's app store. It is likely the app store saved their payment details for future purchases and unless the parent signed out on the child's phone (or even worse, used a password they know), then their child is free to make purchases whenever they like. I have watched children as young as seven use their parent's tablet to go to sites, such as Amazon and make purchases without their parents even knowing.

Whilst technically viruses, like people get on computers, do not exist on smartphones, there is a big threat from malware. This malicious software is often installed by clicking on false links or can even be installed as part of an app. These can be designed to make you visit certain websites (like ads), give a backdoor into someone's phone, send spam or even share some of their details.

Finally, just like with any screen, using smartphones late at night can affect the sleep cycle. The blue light emitted from screens can suppress the release of melatonin in the brain. This sleep drug helps people to feel tired and to regulate their sleep. In addition, the constant receiving of messages and alerts can also desensitise the brain to the feel good drugs as it gets used to the higher levels of awareness (a process called the hedonic treadmill effect). This increased awareness makes people sleep less deeply as their phone pings away throughout the night. Even excessive screen time during the day has been linked to poor sleep in teens.

# Smartphones

The drug *dopamine* is the pleasure-seeking drug that then triggers a release of a natural *opioid* feel-good drug in the brain whenever we get a letter, a present, a message. This drug rewards the brain for the gratification of receiving a message, text or reply.

Unfortunately, what can happen to children (and adults) is that they enter a dopamine loop, where they are seeking the dopamine rush by constantly checking their phone or messages (we all know someone like that) far more than receiving the resulting *opioid* rush. This causes them to spend more time seeking than they are being rewarded, hence a dopamine loop, and it can be a very hard cycle to break. On top of that, the cues that a reward is coming increase the need for dopamine: the ping of a message on their phone, the buzz of the phone vibrating, the light flashing to indicate they have a message. It is very easy to become addicted to waiting for someone to respond to the message someone has just sent.

## The Parent's Guide to the Modern World

| **Dos** | **Don'ts** |
|---|---|
| Discuss the risks with phones, be open and help your child to make the right choices. | Just install software and think it is safe. Spend time searching for how to get around blockers. |
| Invest in phone insurance and protectors. | Rely on your child's phone set up. Education is far more important than dependency on software, as the moment they no longer have the software they will struggle to cope. |
| Teach your child about the risk of image and message sharing. | |
| Do not buy things from your child's phone or enter your card details. | |
| Ensure you log out of the phone's app store. | |
| Teach children how to recognise an advert and not to click on it. | |
| Make sure the setting to warn you or to block potentially dangerous apps is on. | |
| Do not allow phones in the bedroom at night for younger children, and for older children | |

## Smartphones

teach them to turn them off at night.

## Instant Messaging And Chat

As text messaging and sending pictures from mobile to mobile became popular, so the cost of people's bills rose. Therefore, companies started to develop apps to allow messages to be sent through the Internet. Moreover, once Wi-Fi became common in people's homes, this effectively leads to free messaging. It is now possible to send messages, pictures and even videos to each other for free.

Here are some of the most common ones available on all phones and their lower age limit:

> **BBM** (BlackBerry Messenger) - 13+
> A messaging and file-sharing app originally developed for communicating between BlackBerry Smart Phones, however can now be used on all phones. Can add people by email, text, their BlackBerry phone ID (PIN) or even through non-contact via NFC (Near Field Communication) to phones nearby.
>
> **Kik** - 18 or 13+ with parents' permission
> Instant messaging with add-on apps making it possible to connect with different people that are not known to the user.

## Instant Messaging And Chat

**Skype** – 13+

Originally, a free video chat product, it can now be used to message, send video, audio or even files to other users. A more recent feature is the ability to live translate speech. Can message or call people users are not connected with.

**Snapchat** - 13+

Instant messaging of photos, videos, drawings and messages, which then delete themselves after being read. Users can also compile a 'Story', a chronological sequence of photos that can be viewed for 24 hours before they are deleted.

**Surespot**

A free secure instant messaging system. Messages, images and voice recordings can be sent encrypted to another user. Is not linked to a phone number or email address, so can also be used anonymously.

**Viber** – 13+

An instant messaging and calling service that works on phones and computers. Includes the ability to call non-users by buying credit.

**WeChat** - 18 or 13+ with parents' permission

Messaging, calls, broadcasts, video games, location sharing with other users or via Bluetooth. Includes the ability to connect with random users and people who use it near to a user's location.

**WhatsApp** – 16+

An app to send text messages, images, videos, audio and location. It relies on the other person being known to the user and having it installed.

**What are the risks?**

As with social media, one of the big threats to a child is the dangers of online bullying. As some of these apps use identification methods other than phone number in some instances it is possible to send bullying or intimidating messages anonymously once a child's user name or phone number is known.

Grooming is a big thing on instant messaging applications. People are able to reach out to strangers over many of these different apps. It is possible for children to build very trusting relationships by messages and then not realise that they are starting to be asked to do inappropriate things or share images or videos.

Even if a child has not been groomed, they will be going through the ups and downs of social development. This includes the development

## Instant Messaging And Chat

of relationships and sex. It is very common for children to sext (sexualised texting) and share inappropriate pictures or videos of themselves in order to please someone. A child needs to know about this risk, because it is too late once it has happened; the messages or photos are out of a child's hands and can be shared. Even for those apps that show it and then delete it, people can still take screen shots of the image before that happens. Images and videos have been used for bullying, blackmail, pornography, revenge pornography (explicit pictures or videos shared online after a breakup as revenge) and paedophilia.

With some of these apps, they are designed for ease of use. For example, several of the video chat apps have a simple one-touch to start button. This means that potentially they could accidentally take and share images or videos if they do not get into the habit of locking their screen.

## The Parent's Guide to the Modern World

## Instant Messaging And Chat

| **Dos** | **Don'ts** |
|---|---|
| Make sure your child only turns on their Bluetooth and NFC when they want use it. | Give your child unrestricted Internet access. Limit your child's data access to certain hours of the day. |
| Only give your child a smartphone when they are mature enough to be able to talk to you about bullying issues. | Let your child take their phone in their room overnight. |
| Teach your child not to react to any strange or unwanted messages and to report or block them. | |
| Talk to your child about what sexting is and how to deal with anyone who tries to push you into doing something you are not comfortable with. | |
| Help your child to understand that they are likely to be asked for pictures or videos at some point. | |
| Ensure your child knows that you will never be angry with them | |

and that you are there for them to turn to when they experience problems.

# Instant Broadcasting (Livecasting)

Most phones, tablets and laptops have inbuilt video cameras. Originally, these were designed to allow face-to-face communication using software like Skype or FaceTime. More recently, webcams have been used to record video blogs (vlogs), through sites like YouTube, Vimeo, and Facebook. The amount of video content on the Internet is increasing rapidly, to the point where Cisco Visual Networking Index predicts that by 2019 80% of global Internet consumption will be videos. Online seminars, or webinars, have been used for several years as a way of delivering content, live or pre-recorded, to a closed group of attendees.

In more recent years, the concept of live video streaming, or livecasting, has become more common. Users can live broadcast from their device to the service. These videos are then able to be watched live and also replayed for a time afterwards.

This is slightly different to lifestreaming, which is a phenomenon where someone attaches a camera to themselves and can live stream their view to the Internet. Snapchat, Pinterest and Instagram are all similar concepts to this, although predominantly about the sharing of photos.

These are the main instant broadcasting services:

| Service | Minimum age | Length of video availability (unless deleted) |
|---|---|---|
| Google Hangouts/YouTube Live | 13 | Indefinitely (but only public if selected) |
| Instagram (15 second clips) | 13 | Indefinitely |
| Keek | 13 | Indefinitely |
| Meerkat | 12 | - |
| MixBit | 13 | Indefinitely |
| Periscope | 4 | 24 hours |
| Snapchat | 13 | - |
| Tout | 13 | Indefinitely |
| Vine (due to be discontinued) | 17 (there is a child version on iPhones) | Indefinitely |
| YouNow | 13 | 1 week |

## Instant Broadcasting (Livecasting)

**What are the risks?**

It can be very easy to find adult content videos. For example, Periscope has a live stream of videos, which currently includes no restriction on adult broadcasts. Most others forbid the sharing of adult content, such as pornography, however as these are live services, until a video is reported as inappropriate it is very hard to enforce.

Likewise, it is very easy for a child, especially if encouraged to do so by someone online, to broadcast inappropriate videos that could be used for paedophilia, blackmail, bullying, or being downloaded and shared.

## The Parent's Guide to the Modern World

| **Dos** | **Don'ts** |
|---|---|
| Decide what age is appropriate for your child to have an account, most seem to recommend over 13. | Avoid the conversation; it is an easier conversation to have before something happens than afterwards. |
| Ensure that only you can add apps onto their phones. | Be judgemental when something does go wrong; be there for your child. |
| Get involved in videos your child makes. Why not have your own parent/child account? | |
| Talk to your child about the likelihood of someone asking for an inappropriate video from them. | |

# The Internet

The term *Internet* describes the connection of computers around the world. The part of the Internet commonly used is the World Wide Web, a collection of publicly available websites. When we send emails, do online banking or online transactions then we use an area of the Internet called the Deep Web (as it is more secure). The very nature of the Internet means that it holds a number of threats for children, whilst at the same time being one of the most useful resources to help develop them.

# Blogs

Imagine keeping a personal diary online; this is a blog (originally a weblog). There are a number of services that allow people to sign up and start their own blog; this includes sites like Tumblr, Blogger and blog.com. There are a number of different types of blog including personal, business, how-to, reviews, private or opinion. Content on many of these is not monitored. Over the last few years, there has been a huge increase in video blogging (vlogging) through websites like YouTube or Vimeo. These are monitored a lot more closely than written blogs, but also feature a lot more in search results.

**What are the risks?**

As blogs are not heavily monitored, it is very easy to access inappropriate or unsavoury content. For example, a teenager who is self-harming is very able to find blogs with information about how to hide it from parents, how to commit suicide painlessly, non-consensual rape fantasies, bestiality or even how to get a size zero body. Despite the content very often being opinion based, blogs can be written in any style the author chooses. Some are like reading someone's thoughts, others offer step-by-step instructions and some just share other people's content.

The content of people's blogs is public (unless set up otherwise), so therefore is accessible to future employers and also online trolls and bullies. The Internet brings anonymity to people wanting to bully, intimidate or harass people; comments on blogs are the perfect area for these, even in response to perfectly innocent posts. For a child starting a blog set up the comments to require them to be approved.

| Dos | Don'ts |
|---|---|
| As your child grows older, then focus on being an ally and support network for them, be non-judgemental in your approach to helping them (especially during their teenage years). Be the person they turn to for help rather than the blogs. | Rely on your child's Internet history to see what they have been viewing; most Internet browsers have the ability to use the Internet in 'private' mode. |

If your child is starting a blog, prepare them to receive nasty messages.

Young children:

Use parental filters.

Teach them the rule that sites that show people in their underwear or less are for adults and to get you if they see anything like that.

Older children and teenagers

Have an open conversation with them about coping with other people on the Internet and their differing views.

Leave them with an understanding that even if they are on a dodgy site they can come to you for support or advice without being judged.

## Collaborative Sites

The first collaborative website was launched in 1995 as a site for programmers to contribute to a library of different computer code. This was called the WikiWikiWeb (Wiki is Hawaiian for quick), and spawned many other 'wiki' sites to be developed about different topics. The most notable wiki is Wikipedia, which is a publicly written online encyclopaedia, administered mainly by volunteer editors.

Wikis and collaborative websites tend to have very few employees, relying on the public and volunteers to provide and edit the content. Another example that children may frequently access is Reddit. Users submit links to news stories under one of the existing categories on the site. Other users vote it up or down the popularity board.

**What are the risks?**

It does not take much imagining understanding that entries on collaborative websites change frequently and so may not be accurate all of the time. However, there has been many a child (and adult, for example the recent Leveson report into press standards in the UK) who have relied on collaborative sites as sources of information.

## Collaborative Sites

**Dos**

Teach your older child/teenager to check any information they need for academic purposes on other trusted websites prior to putting it in their homework.

**Don'ts**

Copy and paste chunks of text (you or your child).

# Pornography

Since the early days of the Internet, a large proportion of the traffic has always been pornography. It is very easy to access and extremely hard to police. Even innocent searches like 'boy play' can result in adult photos appearing in search results.

Pornography filters provided by Internet Service Providers are not the be all and end all that parents would like them to be. With only a few clicks of a mouse, tech-savvy kids can search for phrases such as 'how to get around pornography filter' and find solutions that mean they are able to bypass the filters.

Some of these bypass methods encourage people to use a series of computers around the world to mask their computer's address, which helps them to access pornography. In worst-case scenarios, these work-arounds tell you how to access the Dark Web, an anonymous area of the Internet known for paedophilia, drugs and pirate downloads.

Parents need to be open with their children about the risks that the Internet poses. Trying to block Internet pornography will only encourage the more determined child to find a way around it. I am sad to say that I have worked with children as young as five who know about pornographic websites and have even been able to differentiate between different types (such as heterosexual and homosexual porn).

## What are the risks?

Excess amounts of pornography can give a skewed interpretation of what is normal during sex. This can have an impact on a child's attitude towards romantic partners and affect their important early sexual encounters. It is important that teenagers understand that what is portrayed does not represent real life. For younger children it normalises sexual acts. This makes it possible that they will act it out in their play or worse, it could be part of the process of being groomed.

It can also have an impact on the chemicals released in the brain. Excessive exposure to the pleasure associated with orgasm from masturbation can 'normalise' the experience and so reduces the amount of dopamine and chemicals released in the brain with orgasm. This leads to a need to seek more extreme stimulation (or pornography) to get the same rush, or indeed the start of the endless search to achieve the rush, although this 'normalises' again with periods of abstinence.

Many pornography websites have adverts on either the page or that pop-up offering connection with people for sex. These are often adverts to paid sites or adult social networks. Scarier are the pop-up windows that appear saying a computer has been infected or a security alert. Often they only have one button and will not close, forcing the user to respond in the way that they want. These can be linked to viruses or malware infecting computers as people click on their links.

# Pornography

| **Dos** | **Don'ts** |
|---|---|
| Make sure your child's technology has up to date anti-virus and malware software on. | Avoid the conversations; your child will come across pornography at some point, it is better to have given them the tools to choose to avoid it. |

**Older children and teenagers:**

Have an open conversation with them about pornography; help them to understand that sex is not as it is depicted on pornographic videos and pictures.

Relax pornography filters, so that your child can get used to unrestricted Internet access before they leave home and do not have you to turn to.

Leave them with an understanding that even if they are on a dodgy site they can come to you for support or advice without being judged.

**Young children:**

Use pornography filters.

Teach them the rule that sites that show people in their underwear or less are for adults and to get you if they see anything like that.

# Hacking

A hacker is someone who seeks or exploits vulnerabilities in computer systems. Children and adults encounter hackers on an almost daily basis and it is important to recognise the ways they access technology to avoid it happening.

**Ways of being hacked:**

> **Trojan horse** – a file that appears to be legitimate and not threatening, but runs silently in the background of a computer, causing nuisance (like continual pop-ups), damage

(deleting or altering files) or giving a hacker backdoor access to a computer.

**Denial of Service** – used to disrupt services by flooding a website with millions of messages or attempts to log on until the computer hosting the website gets so overloaded it freezes and denies anyone service.

**Phishing** – fishing for personal information (like passwords, card details) by using fake links, fake websites, and phone phishing.

**Pharming** – redirecting a genuine web address to a fake one.

**Spoofing** – sending messages pretending to be someone trusted. In extreme cases, the hacker can act as the 'man-in-the-middle' getting emails from two recipients and pretend to be the other one (for example pretend to be Julie emailing Fred, and also Fred emailing Julie).

**Ransomware** – a piece of software that once opened on a computer infects it until a ransom is paid.

**Spyware** – software that sits on a computer and takes an active part in obtaining personal information and could even redirect web browsers to a fake site (tends to be bundled with a software download).

# Hacking

**Brute force attacks** – a hack attack that keeps going until they guess the correct password.

**Password cracking** – unscrambling stored passwords.

**Viruses** – a malicious piece of code that copies itself into documents or applications, which then infects other documents or applications when the first is accessed.

**Worms** – malicious pieces of code burrow and spread without needing to be added to a document or application.

There are several types of hacker; potentially older children and teenagers could be drawn into some of these different motivations. Here are a few of the motivations:

**White Hat** hackers describes people who hack for non-malicious reasons, like testing their own systems.

**Black Hat** hackers are people who hack to disrupt, steal or for personal gain.

**Script kiddies** describes inexperienced hackers who use hacking programs copied off others.

**Hacktivists** are people who hack to achieve a political or ideological objective.

**Cyber terrorists** try to cause terror and fear to further an ideological belief.

State sponsored hackers work for governments.

**Spy hackers** work for businesses or corporations to hack competitors.

## What are the risks?

In today's world, it is important that children understand the risks associated with hacking for several reasons.

Firstly, it is very likely that they will come across some of the different methods described above themselves and so could be victims of hacking. It is important that children are skilled up to recognise what is a phishing email compared to a genuine one, for example. The protection of personal data is fundamental to Internet safety, such as having different passwords so that the hacking of one does not mean loss of large amounts of data. One of the biggest threats to the security of online data is people's laziness with passwords, they either go for simple easily guessable ones or they use the same password on a variety of different sites. The latter poses the biggest threat as hacking one site gives someone access to a whole chain of sites; the most important being an email account, as this is where we store much of our login data and also where the hackers would receive emails resetting passwords for other sites.

# Hacking

It can be very easy to find basic steps to hack websites, feeding into the dopamine/opioid loop that drives people to seek and then get pleasure from seeking. The young brain is more susceptible to getting into dopamine loops, where they are not satisfied by the success and so seek more, making the act of hacking more addictive for some children. This could lead to peer pressure if one of their friends has downloaded some software or learnt some simple computer programming to begin hacking. It may even begin very innocently with a child looking up the code to 'hack' into a game to help them to cheat to win it. There are many high profile examples of teenagers hacking websites, such as the teenager alleged to have hacked 259 websites in 90 days in 2012; in another example, two teenagers were arrested over the hacking of the website belonging to a large mobile phone provider in the UK.

## The Parent's Guide to the Modern World

| Dos | Don'ts |
|---|---|
| Check links on suspicious emails by hovering over them and looking at the link address (often in the bottom left of the browser) to make sure they match. | Let your child become a hacker through peer pressure. Educate them enough that they can make their own moral choices and turn to you for advice when they need it. |
| Teach teenagers to look at the 'From' address of emails to check it looks right. | Let your child have the same password for different sites. |
| Teach your child how to safely use a pop-up blocker to choose which sites are safe to let windows appear. | Let your child know your passwords. |
| Use up-to-date virus software, scan your devices regularly and teach your child to consider scans a regular chore. | |

# Pirated Software, Music And Films

Illegal copies of computer programs, music and films are easy to source on the Internet. People very often upload copies of music, films or programmes to video sharing sites like YouTube. These often infringe copyright laws and are frequently removed at the request of the copyright owners. This then forces people seeking free versions to find other means. Historically this may have been through illegal copies sold in the community, however the Internet now gives us access to illegal downloads relatively easily.

Websites have been set up to allow users to upload files for others to download, or more frequently websites that host *Torrents*. Torrents are files that contain information about where to download files from. This means that an illegal copy of a game could be split into a number of different files and hosted on different computers, a *Torrent* can then be uploaded that means when it is accessed, all of these different locations are loaded and the files downloaded. Many Torrent sites claim not to be breaking laws, as they do not host the illegal copies themselves, they are just hosting the data of the locations of these files.

**What are the risks?**

It is very easy (just download a piece of software) to set a home computer up as a host for files accessed by Torrents. This in effect shares a folder on the computer with the public. In theory the rest of the contents of the computer are safe, however some Torrent software can contain *Trojan Horses*, *Malware* or *Spyware*. These could potentially open up back doors into the computer or record personal details.

Most people who contribute to hosting Torrents are doing so as they want to share a game/video/music, however there are people who make money out of Torrents by uploading fake or infected files.

Several high profile legal actions have been taken against Torrent sites, in addition to users sharing or downloading the pirated copies; for minors this could include the parents. Tracking the user can be harder in the case of anonymous downloads via the Dark Web, another reason a child may end up using a *Torbrowser* to access the Dark Web (see the next chapter).

## Pirated Software, Music And Films

| **Dos** | **Don'ts** |
|---|---|
| As with many things about the Internet, the key here is to have an open relationship with your child, so that when they get into difficulties they will come to you for help. | Rely on your child knowing to make the right choice; it is very easy to find download links for pirated content and very tempting for your child. |
| Teach your teenager how to see virus and malware scanning as regular good housekeeping. | |
| Make sure your child knows the risks and recognises the warning signs (pop ups, heavy ads, new icons appearing after a download). | |

## The Dark Web

There are different levels of the Internet that we use for different reasons. Webpages and sites you look at normally are at the surface level of the World Wide Web. However, the Internet is different, as this describes the connecting of computers around the world. There are other areas of the Internet used by people, not just the World Wide Web.

An example would be when doing banking online, people log in through their computers or smartphones and the information they view is strictly between their device and the bank's. When people send emails they go via part of the Internet, but are not displayed or accessible on the World Wide Web. At this deeper level of the Internet (known as the Deep Web), more secure transactions take place. As security increases (for example military agencies), they use the deepest levels of the Deep Web because they have increased levels of security.

The Dark Web lies beyond the Deep Web. To access this most secure part of the Internet, users log in anonymously through a random chain of computers across the Internet. These are called Tor Servers and by logging in using special software, people anonymously connect to one computer or server, this then connects them to another, and another, and another... Until in the end, the user cannot be tracked back through the complex daisy chain (especially if they have added

## The Dark Web

further security software to their computer). This anonymity makes it a breeding ground for child pornography websites, drugs exchanges and other illegal transactions.

**What are the risks?**

The biggest threat to a teenager or a child is that parents will not be able to tell what they are accessing or be able to block it. As the daisy chain they connect to every time changes, the moment they stop them connecting to one server, then the software connects to another. The reality is that education is the only form of stopping this.

It is very easy to access the Dark Web; you just download the Tor software and connect. A child could easily have it recommended to them as a place to download illegal copies of music, games or films, for example. If this is the case, then it will not show up on an Internet log, as this will be a log of things accessed via the World Wide Web. They are not accessing the Dark Web via the World Wide Web so it will not show.

## Dos

Discuss it with your child; they need to know what it is and how easy it is to be sucked in.

Be open about the dangers it poses to them, teach them to recognise when they are not comfortable on a site.

Be open to talking through your child's social problems, at some point one of their friends is likely to mention Tor and this is how you will be more likely to hear about it.

## Don'ts

Try and block it, you will get frustrated with trying and your child will spend more time working out how to get around the systems you put in place.

# The Internet of Things

There are millions of devices around the world that connect to the Internet or local networks, such as home Wi-Fi. There are many practical reasons for inanimate objects to be able to communicate with other machines. For example, roads that can sense when there is a traffic jam, which then communicate with surrounding traffic lights to ease the flow of traffic. In the future of self-driving cars, they could then communicate with cars in the area. Another example could be a vending machine that automatically places the order for restocking.

People can wear smart bracelets or watches that provide information to their phone or computer on their activity, or vice versa. Currently associated with fitness regimens, smart bracelets could potentially offer health monitoring for those with heart problems. In addition, smartwatches are being released that allow people to interact with their phones or read messages on their wrists.

Honestly dear, it was the Fridge that restocked itself with all this beer!

In homes, people can now get central heating systems that they can control from their phones. It is possible to remotely control devices, like baby cameras, in different parts of homes. People can print things wirelessly, stream television from a device to a television and much more.

**What are the risks?**

There are large security concerns around the Internet of Things, with many devices having little or no security and many using the default passwords. There are search engines set up to find devices local to an area or to search for particular types of device. It is possible to watch live feeds from people's unsecured cameras with a few clicks of the mouse.

Changing the manufacturer's password is critical when using devices that connect to the Internet of Things. Aside from other people being able to access them (as we have seen above), it is also possible to easily hack them otherwise. A particular manufacturer will often have a default password for its devices, so provided that is known (and is often shown on the manufacturer's website) then hacking a device is easy if the password has not been changed.

In fact, it is so easy to do that potentially a child might even find it fun or a game. Because they could achieve success quite quickly, they may then start searching for something that is a bit more of a challenge. As they move up the hacking scale, it can very easily become addictive as the brain is pumped full of dopamine, the searching drug, seeking the reward from the achievement of cracking something.

# The Parent's Guide to the Modern World

| **Dos** | **Don'ts** |
|---|---|
| Think carefully about what devices your child connects to the Internet. | Leave default passwords on. |
| Be open to talking about how easy it can be to crack default passwords and why you should change them. | |
| Help your child to feel success without the need to hack. | |

# Social Media

Social media describes online software or applications to help with our communication and sharing of information with others. Accessible from computers or devices, like phones, much communication takes place in written form rather than face-to-face or by telephone.

This brings its own challenges as humans rely on so many signals other than just words; we use intonation and facial expression to understand the hidden meanings of what someone is saying. Even handwritten notes convey hidden meanings; the size of text, the neatness, the flow and style of the writing all tell the reader something about the context of the message contained in the words on the page. Emotion icons, known as emoji, are often used as an indicator of the context of the message. Acronyms like LOL (laugh out loud or lots of love) or ROFL (roll on floor laughing) can also be used to ensure that the nature of the message is not misread.

The Parent's Guide to the Modern World

Social media is also immediate; people send a message and it can be seen anywhere in the world immediately. Far more, for our young people, the temptation is to reply to a message they have received straight away. This means that they can respond with their emotions without regard for consequence, a common cause of social difficulty for teenagers who lack the ability to understand how the person might receive the message. Combine that with the effects of dopamine, the brain is seeking hormone, and children are growing up with an increasing need to be satisfied as immediately as they can.

# Trolling And Online Bullying

One of the biggest things that the current age has done is move social activities online. This means that many of the friendship groups and social engagements that were experienced in the playground or out playing now take place online. Unfortunately, this also includes bullying, not just the seemingly harmless name-calling that many people did as youngsters; this can be serious and prolonged from an individual or a group. Trolling, specifically Internet trolling is the practice of posting comments or remarks that are offensive, aggressive or disruptive to the conversation.

The reason is threefold - the Internet allows people to be anonymous, the Internet puts words into print or pictures, the Internet removes inhibitions.

Being anonymous or taking over someone's identity allows people to hide behind a mask and intimidate or bully online. As many sign-up processes online are automated, it is very easy to either create fraudulent or fake accounts. To create a fraudulent email

account only takes a few personal details about the person, such as their gender and where they live. Other things like date of birth, pet's name and other personal data can often be stolen from social media, such as someone's (or their relative's) Facebook page. Once they have these details they are able to taken over other social media accounts, using the personal information to reset the password and change the email address on the account. It is easy to set up fake accounts, by again beginning with an email address, which only requires a phone number for verification. Again, from here it is easy to then set up fake profiles on social media.

Even without anonymity people will often post or make unkind comments on social media. Celebrities and people in the spotlight are often the focus for Internet trolling, however with teens the target can often be other children. Peer pressure and gang culture may amplify this, with children sometimes being subjected to comments and ridicule from multiple others. Even innocuous comments, which if said as part of a conversation would be let go, are there for our minds to keep revisiting.

The Internet allows people's inhibitions to be removed; very often people will comment on posts or forums with seemingly little or no regard for the impact. They do not see the reaction of the person receiving the message and often do not know them personally, so do not need to moderate themselves. The brain tricks them into thinking there will be no effect, because it is not the same as saying it to someone's face, or that it is inconsequential. The little thoughts that everyone has inside their minds can be posted online quicker than the other voices in their heads react telling them to stop.

## What are the risks?

It is very easy to slip into trolling. It is different to bullying, which tends to be a more directed attack on an individual on multiple occasions. It is then easy to move from making incongruent comments that go against a post or conversation (Internet trolling) to it becoming a campaign or regular occurrence (bullying). To be a victim of bullying is a matter of perception; if the individual is secure in their own self-identity and resilient enough to walk away and not be affected by the campaign, even if by a group, then they are unlikely to be a victim of bullying. However, if someone feels insecure, depressed or anxious then they may more likely focus on the comments or take them to heart. This can lead to further insecurity, depression, paranoia or vulnerability.

Unlike in-person bullying and intimidation, which can often be left behind by walking away, social media reminds us of its presence. Social media will inform users they have a new comment, notify them when they log in. In the case of someone who is being bullied or feels picked on by the comments or replies, then this adds a level of fear and dread to the receiving of notifications.

The hormones released in the brain cause a fight, flight, freeze response in the body and also secrete pheromones in the sweat, causing the so-called smell of fear. The same process that helps us to love now links emotional pain to an experience. This will cause a sense of dread whenever notifications are received, but also the dopamine boost that makes it almost irresistible to not read it.

## Trolling And Online Bullying

| **Dos** | **Don'ts** |
|---|---|
| From a young age, teach your child to walk away from people who say unkind things. | Assume your child would not troll someone, it is very easy to do and they may not realise how their words are received. |
| As your teen starts to use social media, teach them to always stop and think before posting comments, photos or videos. | |
| Be open to listening to your child's experiences without judging, they need to know they are safe coming to you with their problems. | |

## Facebook

Facebook is a social networking service that launched in 2004. It was originally designed to help students at Harvard University communicate with each other and its development and worldwide success has been the subject of feature film *The Social Network*.

People over the age of 13 are able to sign up for free to connect with 'Friends', publish updates about what they are doing, share photos or videos, join groups of people with shared interests or even 'Follow' updates from companies or celebrities. Users complete a profile giving details of themselves, their interests and hobbies; the profile also shows their published posts (called a status), photos and videos depending on the security settings for each. There are a number of apps that can be added to each user's Facebook, such as games, many of which are free, but encourage users to invite 'Friends' to use them, include adverts or purchase upgrades.

Facebook centres on a timeline, where posts, photos and videos from 'Friends' and also 'Liked' interests, groups or pages appear. There are often so many that they do not all appear, so these often change within seconds. Users are able to 'Like' (indicate you like or agree with a post), comment or even share posts to their profile timeline for their Friends to see. Advertisements appear in your timeline and on the side of the timeline when viewed on a computer.

# Facebook

Facebook have recently launched a version for use in school communities, called Lifestage. It focuses on sharing videos and pictures with classmates for them to either like or dislike. Users are unable to chat on this app, however everything that is shared can be viewed by anyone in the school's group (which people can add themselves to) and the app warns that videos are public.

**What are the risks?**

Facebook's ability to connect with other people across the world gives a fantastic opportunity for children; however, it can also lead to an incredible number of social and relationship problems that they may not have the skills to cope with.

Just like with many other forms of social media, posts, photos and videos can be shared very easily. Even with privacy settings, it is still easy to take a screen shot of an image, for example, and send it to others. Many users have been caught out with photos or posts that they did not realise were public rather than restricted to their Friends or a segment of their list. Public posts, images and videos can be viewed by anyone, even those who do not have a Facebook account, such as potential future employers, for example.

Although against Facebook rules, it is possible to set up accounts in false names or with fake profiles. For example, they could set up an account in the name of a real person and impersonate them. Hackers with fake profiles can, by becoming your Friend, get many of your personal details, such as pets, parents' names, date of birth, or email address. This gives them information to be able to answer security questions, for example. Some people setting up fake profiles get very complex and have entire networks of made-up friends too; there may even be a complex story to go along with them.

Facebook may be used as a way of approaching people who are strangers without adding them as a Friend by requesting permission to message them. Facebook's chat facility (which is also available as its own Instant Messaging app for phones) allows Friends to message each other privately. If a non-Friend wants to message someone it sends him or her a request to talk, which they can accept or delete. As with many of the instant messaging apps, children need to be aware of the dangers of talking to strangers online and the risk of grooming.

By far the biggest issue with social media is the impact it can have on friendships, social lives and relationships. Bullies and trolls will often respond to posts, habitually not caring about the impact of their

## Facebook

comments. It is common for people to use social media to be very vocal about taking a different stance and also use posts as an opportunity to insult or try to injure someone's feelings. Facebook can cause a whole number of social and relationship problems through comments, sharing of posts and online chat.

## Dos

Make sure your child is old enough to understand about the different privacy levels for their posts, images and videos, so that they can make informed choices about each one they post.

Help your child to add new Friends to different lists, so they can share things with their different segments (e.g. school friends, work, family etc.).

Be a non-judgemental sounding board for your child's social problems, listen and help guide them.

Teach your child to only add people they know.

## Don'ts

Try to wade in with social problems.

Rely on your child knowing when not to reply; you learned how to walk away rather than respond to something, so does your child.

# MySpace

MySpace is a social networking site known for its ability to share music and videos. Users are able to create their own radio station, a playlist of music, write updates on their bulletin board, message other users and post videos. Part owned by musician Justin Timberlake and relaunched in 2013, it was larger than Facebook and more visited than Google in the past.

Users create a profile where they display a brief bio, their location, a social wall where they and others can post messages, links, photos or videos. They also have separate pages on their profile to display uploaded pictures and videos, plus create their own music playlists.

**What are the risks?**

As the focus of MySpace is on music, unlike Facebook or Twitter, users focus on common interests, such as bands. It is therefore likely that children will connect with people who they do not know. Just the same as in other social media, this means that for potential groomers it could be easy to connect. By showing similar interests as a child, they could start a friendship that they use to groom them over a period of time.

It is possible that MySpace can be used for bullying and trolling, using a child's profile to target them or their choice of music. Posts, profiles and comments can be easily reported. MySpace's Report Abuse page encourages minors to talk to their parent, teacher or a trusted adult.

# MySpace

**Dos**

Make sure your child is wary of any connections they do not know trying to chat in private.

Show your teen how to report abuse.

**Don'ts**

Think of it just as a music-sharing site, the social communication aspect of this site (and app) make it a real threat.

## Twitter

Twitter is a form of social media that is all about sharing thoughts, messages or news in less than 140 characters. The concept is that people follow (or subscribe) to see the 'Tweets' (posted messages) that other people post. Tweets users write can be seen in the news feed of everyone who is following them. Many users who want to write longer Tweets will often put 1/3, 2/3, 3/3 at the end to signify it is a multipart message. Photos and videos can also be shared on Twitter.

Twitter terms allow anyone over 13 to sign up. People choose their username, or a Twitter handle; this begins with an @ symbol. Their Profile Photo (the square picture that appears alongside any posts they make) and their header photo (the photo across the top of the page when someone looks at their profile) are public. There are a number of settings like the ability to 'Protect my Tweets' – allowing users to approve the request of other people to view your Tweets. This feature only works in the future, it does not back date, so any Tweets done without turning on privacy can be viewed publicly.

To engage someone in a public conversation in Twitter all users have to do is tag them in their Tweet by including their @ username, for example '@thekidcalmer I read your article, it was so helpful!' They will then normally receive a notification of an interaction and they can choose to reply (by including the original user's @ username in their

## Twitter

Tweet, for example '@confidentparent Thank you, glad it helped you') or by clicking the reply arrow below their Tweet. If someone agreed with, enjoyed or liked the other person's Tweet they can 'Like' it by clicking the heart icon below the Tweet, or 'Retweet' it by clicking the squared arrow logo below a Tweet. Users can just choose to share other people's Tweets or 'Quote' it and add a few comments of their own (for example 'Such kind words from @confidentparent. @thekidcalmer I read your article it was so helpful!'). To privately message other Twitter users, both must be following each other unless the account is set up to receive messages from others. There is a feature to accept message requests from people users are not following in the Settings.

Because of its nature, Twitter is used a lot by celebrities for interaction with fans and to share details of their daily lives. This has made them a lot more accessible to the public and depending on the celebrity, it is common to get a Retweet or even a reply.

**What are the risks?**

Twitter reinforces the subliminal messages of sharing everything that happens in our lives. To most people this is fine, as they know where to draw a line; however, children are less likely to have that constraint. For most mundane things, this is fine, but consider if they start posting about their relationships, or even that their parents are away and they are going to have a party.

Online bullying is also a threat, where potentially false (or even real) accounts can be used to publicly tag a child in offensive Tweets. Twitter offers the ability to Mute (so you do not see Tweets from that user), Block (blocking interaction with that user) or Report (tell Twitter about an offensive Tweet) Tweets by clicking on the three dots under a Tweet.

Grooming potentially is possible on Twitter, but would likely occur by someone interacting with a child publicly at first and then swapping over to private messages at some time.

| Dos | Don'ts |
|---|---|
| Make sure 'Protect My Tweets' is on when your child signs up. | Spy on them. |
| Make sure your child's account cannot receive message requests from people they do not follow (in Settings). | Join Twitter just to follow them. |
| Teach your child to only allow people to follow them they know. | |
| Ensure that the Photo Tagging feature is set to 'Only allow people I follow to tag me in photos'. | |
| Teach them to use the Mute, Block or Report features and to tell you about bullying, harassment or inappropriate comments. | |

## Pinterest and Instagram

Instagram is an online photo-sharing site, where users can share their photos or up to 15 seconds of video. Registered users are able to comment and 'like' (and report) other people's images and videos. Users upload pictures from their device and are able to apply various effects to their photo (for example to make it black or white), adding a comment and upload it to the web. Instagram can be linked to other forms of social media, like Twitter and Facebook.

Pinterest is less of a social media platform; it is a creative photo-sharing platform. The concept is that users share creative ideas and links to interesting websites. People then create their own 'Pinboards' to collect useful ideas together, just like in real life you may stick notes up and cut out adverts onto a pinboard for easy reference. Pinterest have also introduced a messaging facility to communicate with other users.

Registration for these sites is restricted to over 13 and whilst it will be possible to share inappropriate pictures, they are likely to be noticed very quickly and removed.

## What are the risks?

Whilst comments and profiles can contain links to inappropriate websites, the largest risk is the threat of online bullying through comments or photos. For example, just like with other social media, bullies could try to intimidate with innocuous photos of a teen's house, their bedroom window or places they go. If this is combined with some in-person or online comments this could be very scary for a child.

Potentially there are the usual concerns about personal information being shared too. For example, content could be used to become familiar with where a child lives, their habits and interests or even what pets they have. For a groomer this is valuable information, as they will want to appear to have similar tastes or interests to a child as they build up their trust.

## Dos

Teach your child to report inappropriate posts or comments and to be able to ignore them.

Tell your child to watch out for people they do not know wanting to have private or offline conversations.

## Don'ts

Rely on your child to not post too much personal information, be open to talking about the threats online.

# Immersive Technology And Experiences

## Virtual Reality

Virtual reality is the concept of being able to enter an imaginary world created by technology. Currently this is achieved by wearing goggles or headsets with a screen in or a mobile phone slotted in. The device recognises which way the user is facing and adjusts the image on the screen to give the user a 360° view, in addition to the ability to look up and down. Current devices have onscreen menus; the user moves their head to highlight the button they want to select and they use the one button to click.

However, this is just the beginning of what is possible. The technology to create surround sound already exists. Digital scent technology has existed since the 1950s when Smell-O-Vision and AromaRama developed technology to release smells as a film was showing. Although ultimately doomed, this showed the interest in immersive experiences and computer generated smells began to be developed in the 1990s. It will not be long before the other senses follow.

**What are the risks?**

Human eyes are not used to focussing on screens so near to their faces, so children are likely to be prone to the side effects of eye fatigue or strain. For years, people have been used to looking at screens a couple of metres away in the corner of the room, then this transferred to screens on a desk, to screens on laps and in people's hands. Adults recognise when their eyes are tired and know when to take a walk, make coffee or do something else. This is a skill that is hard for children to recognise and very few have the internal skills to know how to deal with it, just think how hard it is to get a child off the computer.

Symptoms of eye strain:

> Headaches,
> Blurred vision,

> Difficulty focussing,
>
> Tiredness,
>
> Sore or itchy eyes,
>
> Watery or dry eyes.

Unfortunately, these sensations can also lead a child to become more determined to finish something, more frustrated when they do not then complete their game and subsequently more determined to complete the game. It becomes an eyestrain loop that is hard for adults to break, let alone children.

As Virtual Reality is immersive, it can trick the brain into thinking that the experiences are real. For example, rollercoaster simulations can give some users the sick feeling that is caused by the movement, despite them not actually moving. For children this is huge, as they will be experiencing the same emotions and sensations that they would encounter by doing the activity in real life.

The blue light emitted from screens delays the release of *melatonin* in the brain. *Melatonin* is the drug that helps regulate sleep pattern, helping the brain to feel tired in the evenings as the darkness falls, telling the body to prepare for sleep, reducing the production of urine during the night and helping to wake the body up in the morning. As many early VR headsets are based on using phones for the images, these are bad offenders for emitting blue light.

# The Parent's Guide to the Modern World

| **Dos** | **Don'ts** |
|---|---|
| For young children put a time limit on their use of VR. | Let your child use VR headsets late at night. |
| Teach your child how to recognise the symptoms of eyestrain from middle childhood. | Minimise the emotional and physical sensation of the experience, your child may need your support to cope with the after-effects. |
| Show your child how you recognise your eyes are getting tired and comment on how you are choosing to walk away. | |

Virtual cleaning is so much easier.

# 3D Printing

3D printers are a huge technological advance; the ability to print objects from a computer file has revolutionised many problems around the world. For example, it is possible to send a 3D printer to one area of the planet and then get it to print other 3D printers. The printers can produce composite parts for making more complex mechanical objects and have even been used to make prosthetic limbs, such as working hands.

As 3D printers get cheaper and so become more widespread, then the way items are repaired, replaced and purchased will change hugely, people will buy a plan for something and not have to wait for delivery as they print it themselves.

**What are the risks?**

It has not taken long for people to try to abuse 3D printing, with various attempts being reported in the media to try to create a working gun. The first firing gun made from a 3D printer was reported in the United States in May 2013. Likewise, the sex trade has already found uses for the technology.

The possibility of 3D printing drugs is also just starting to be explored, with the US Food and Drug Administration approving the first 3D printed pill in August 2015. Once this becomes more widely adopted then it is easy to foresee this being used in the illegal drugs trade, immediately solving many of the trafficking issues that drugs gangs have.

As with many other risks for children, peer pressure and friendships will play a part of the threats around 3D printers. Downloading a particular plan for something might be a reason for a child to be attracted to the Dark Web, for example. Friends may challenge each other or decide it would be cool to print a gun or something similar, because potentially deadly as it may be, they may just see it as a toy they print.

## 3D Printing

| **Dos** | **Don'ts** |
|---|---|
| Talk with your teenager about the humanistic benefits of 3D printing and the changes it could bring to the world. | Expect a child to understand the importance of 3D printing, when they first start to use it, it will be a fun activity to print toys or similar. This is fine at this stage as it is part of exploration of new technology, however set a boundary for what they can and cannot print right from the start. |
| If you get a 3D printer, then initially have some way of monitoring or controlling its use. Discuss what it is and is not to be used for. | |

## Brain-Computer Interfaces

Recently on television, viewers witnessed a celebrity driving a car with just their brain! Interfaces that read brain activity can be used to fly remote controlled helicopters or control lighting. Other technology that can be controlled from a brain-computer interface include game characters, phones, apps, a robotic arm, moving furry ears (!) and music playlists.

These devices do not read people's minds or brain waves, what they do is register brain activity in certain parts of the brain. The clearer these are, the easier it is to control these devices. To begin with, users are asked to focus on thinking about one thing; the more they focus, the more the device registers and the unit responds. It takes many hours of practice to perfect control, but once this can be accomplished, the ability to control devices with your brain becomes quite simple.

# Brain-Computer Interfaces

## What are the risks?

Brain-controlled devices rely on the ability to have clarity of thought. Children living in the modern world have many distractions and will often crave lots of stimulation. They will often be doing several things at the same time and flick from one thing to another. When they are doing homework, they will often be watching TV or doing something else at the same time. Even if not, they will flick from one screen to another or be chatting to someone online.

This technology will also help gaming, with developers already linking the colours of a light to the brain activity as they play. They are looking at ways of linking that with recordings of game play. When that is the case, it is likely to at least triple the length of game play, as they play, watch their play and then re-play.

| **Dos** | **Don'ts** |
|---|---|
| Help your child to clear their mind and focus on one thing.<br><br>Single tasking is key; teach your child the benefits on focusing on something singly for shorter periods. | Be heavy handed with taking away technology as your child does their homework; if they're used to flicking between things they'll need a gentle approach to getting used to more focus. |

# Interactive Eyewear

Interactive eyewear means glasses that show information or allow a wearer to interact with information displayed on the inside on the lenses. These were thought to be the thing of fantasy until, in April 2012, Google announced Google Glass, prototype interactive eyewear. Initially they were only available in the US, but in 2014 they went on sale for $1,500. They were subsequently withdrawn from sale in January 2015 amidst security concerns, however Google state they are committed to continuing to develop them. There was even a research project to assess their use in healthcare (for example for surgeons) undertaken in Europe. There was also a trial of using them with breastfeeding mothers in Australia, showing (via a secure link) information on the screen about common breastfeeding problems.

Interactive eyewear or smart glasses are on the increase; some contain a small screen, and others project an image onto the lenses to give the appearance of a holographic image. They can be controlled by touchpads, buttons, speech recognition, gesture recognition (for example typing on an imaginary keyboard), eye tracking or even brain-computer interfaces.

Development of interactive eyewear is very much a work in progress; Wikipedia lists 18 different projects in development, so expect to see this technology available in the next few years.

**What are the risks?**

One of the risks that were identified during the public trials of Google Glass was the risk of eye pain or eyestrain. As with Virtual Reality, human eyes are not trained for focussing on things so close to their eyes, so it is important that children have learnt how to recognise eye strain, how to walk away from technology when they recognise it and not to get frustrated and throw or break their interactive eyewear.

As a reminder, the symptoms of eyestrain are:

> Headaches,
> Blurred vision,
> Difficulty focussing,
> Tiredness,
> Sore or itchy eyes,
> Watery or dry eyes.

A large area of concern in the public has been around privacy issues surrounding the use of smart glasses. Concerns could include if the glasses are listening in on conversations, recording or even broadcasting them. There was even a reported account of a woman in a San Francisco bar being attacked because of these concerns as she was wearing interactive glasses and the attackers' privacy was being invaded. In certain countries, they would be illegal, due to the possibility that they can record in an inconspicuous manner (for example taking a photograph by just winking).

Another risk with interactive eyewear is their security settings and whether they are vulnerable to being hacked. They connect via Wi-Fi or Bluetooth, so it could be very easy to access them that way, for example (just as you can browse files on other computers on the same computer network in an office or home). There have been reports that as users type their passwords on a virtual keyboard, this can be recorded or interpreted to give away their password. Another hacker claimed to be able to hijack smartglasses by getting a user to view a QR code (a square-based barcode).

Finally, there are concerns about the impact of distraction for the user, for example, when being worn whilst driving (whether on or off). This concern is around possible restriction of view, but also of the distraction of information or messaging on the glasses.

| **Dos** | **Don'ts** |
|---|---|
| Teach your child the symptoms of eyestrain. | Ignore this as a technology that is just a dream, it is likely to be available in retail stores in just a few years. |
| From an early age, get your child used to knowing there is a time and a place for technology, so that they are in healthy habits of choice before smartglasses are commercially available. | |

# Speech Recognition

Speech recognition has been researched as far back as the 1950s, if not earlier; it has developed enormously and is now common in many different technologies, such as phones, cars and even helicopters.

Speech recognition software is being used to help people develop their speech, helping them to improve their pronunciation and fluency. It can be used with those who have limited or no sight to enable them to write and is widely used with people who suffer from dyslexia.

Many phones have speech recognition in their own personal assistant software. Apple phones famously have Siri, for example, who will search and attempt to answer any questions people have or undertake simple tasks like calling people. There is other voice-controlled software out there, which are also covered in the Artificial Intelligence section.

**What are the risks?**

It is regions of the frontal lobes that deal with speech, whereas written communication is processed through the parietal lobes. As the brain shuts down the frontal lobes during puberty, it could have an impact on their use of speech recognition software. For example, if they use it a lot with their homework, then they may effectively have to learn new skills to cope during puberty to overcome the shutting off of the frontal lobes. This also explains why some children are able to text and talk at the same time: they have engaged different parts of their brain.

Speech recognition is used in some games, and there are some anecdotal reports of it being affected by people's accents (or possibly by illness too). This could lead to increased levels of frustration or even shouting from a child as they try to get the game to do as they want.

Using speech recognition software whilst trying to do something else (for example drive) can be a distraction. Part of this is to do with the need to check what the software has recognised or repeat the same name again and again and again until the phone recognises that you want it to call Tim. The other part is that, whilst speech is processed

## Speech Recognition

in the frontal lobes, the information that is received back, the text people listen to, the message they are dictating, are all received in the same central region of the brain as all of the other pieces of information to do with the other activity a person is doing (for example driving). Their brain will be trying to differentiate all of the separate pieces of information at the same time.

## Dos

Teach your child to use the technology wisely; if they are meant to be doing something important, like homework, at the same time, then they should focus more intently on that for a shorter period of time. This is then a transferable skill when it comes to distractions whilst driving.

Help your child to recognise frustration and how to walk away/calm down, rather than react. As they grow and things, such as speech recognition software, frustrate them, it will not then be made worse by them getting frustrated.

## Don'ts

Assume your child will know when to use speech recognition; they will want to consume it. Teach them to make decisions about whether it is the best thing to use.

# Gesture Recognition

In 2002, Tom Cruise starred in a film called *Minority Report*. In that futuristic film, Cruise's team of police used people's minds and technology to predict serious crime. One of the most awe-inspiring technologies they used was the glass screen that they used to bring up computer files and pictures and then moved them around just using their hand gestures. That technology exists today and can be seen in devices like the Wii.

This can be incredibly complex and relies on devices interpreting the intention of the gesture. There are three types of gesture: deictic (pointing at something, for example 'can I sit there?' can be communicated through a pointing gesture); mimetic (communicating meaning by moving to represent the shape of an object, such as someone miming drinking from a cup as an offer of a drink) and arbitrary gestures (gestures that communicate something that needs to be learnt, such as thumbs up for well done).

There are six different ways of a computer recognising gestures:

> **Single camera** – moving a part of your body to a particular area of the screen, to click a button for example. Software is being developed to allow 2D cameras to recognise hand gestures.

**Two (stereo) cameras or infrared sensors** – this allows a 3D image to track the gestures and compare them to pre-existing algorithms.

**Depth cameras** – still in development, but these will be 2D cameras (possibly combined with infrared cameras) to develop a rough 3D image.

**Wired gloves** – gloves that are wired to track hand movements.

**Controllers** – hand held controllers, which are tracked by receivers, such as mice, Wii remotes, joysticks and so on.

**Radar** – scientists are currently working (and have demonstrated prototypes) on installing miniature radars into devices that allow hand and finger movements to control operations, such as volume.

## What are the risks?

With the development of this technology, there have been a number of games created to promote physical exercise (such as the Wii Fit add-on). Whilst this promotes physical activity for a child, there are many parents whose teens are using it as an excuse not to be outside (getting vital vitamin D) or telling them they have done some when they have not.

Potentially, this software could prove difficult to use for those with physical impairment or disability. However, as with Professor Stephen Hawking, it could enable someone to succeed as they learn to use the technology. The risk could be that they become frustrated by the fact the computer cannot recognise their movements; or vice versa, they could self-limit and opt-out from using it when it will help them to overcome aspects of their disability.

## The Parent's Guide to the Modern World

| **Dos** | **Don'ts** |
|---|---|
| Make sure that if your child has a device, like a Wii, that they develop disciplines to keep space free for using it. | If your child has a physical disability, do not let them avoid gesture recognition software. |
| Ensure your teenager does spend time outside, even if they are using fitness games on their devices. | |

# Gaming

Immersive technology would not be complete without talking about gaming. Computer games began with simple games, such as Spacewar or Pong, where play was simply directional with a single button to fire/engage/start. Interestingly this is also the stage that simple Virtual Reality games are at currently.

Computer games can be accessed on a wide variety of technology, from computers, tablets, phones to customised gaming machines, such as the Wii, Xbox or PlayStation. Many of these now rely on Internet connection and rather than loading games from a CD, they can be purchased (or illegally downloaded) from the Internet.

Types of games:

**Sandbox** (or Open World) – sandbox games have no objective; they just provide a platform for the player to create their own world/objectives, just as they would in a sandpit. Examples include Minecraft, Grand Theft Auto or Assassin's Creed.

**Simulation** – games that allow the player to simulate the use of vehicles (for example flight simulators), real-life (such as The Sims or virtual pets), or construction (such as city or theme park building).

**Role-play** – a game where the player role-plays a character through a narrative adventure to save the world or society. Dungeons and Dragons, The Witcher and Diablo are a few examples of this large genre.

**Adventure** – similar to role playing games, however adventure games take the single player on a quest to solve a problem, using problem solving skills, dialogue with game characters and the gathering of objects, tools and weapons.

**Fighting** – games where the purpose is to make your character fight an opponent, such as Mortal Kombat, Street Fighter and Tekken.

**Action** – a game that requires hand-eye coordination and motor skills to complete levels or tasks. Examples include level games, such as Sonic The Hedgehog or Mario Bros. (which are still going.)

**Shooter** – games where the objective is to complete levels by shooting people. Usually these are from a first person viewpoint so the player does not see their character, just their hands or weapon. These can also be played with others, either in person or over the Internet.

**Strategy** – a game that requires the player to strategize to complete the task/level. Games like chess, Command and Conquer or Civilisation all require real-time strategy thinking to complete.

**Card or board games** – computerised versions of classic card or board games, such as Solitaire, Mah-jong, Monopoly or Cluedo.

**Puzzles/brain games** – games that have a series of levels with problems to solve, such as Angry Birds, Bejeweled or Tetris.

**Sports** – computerised versions of sporting activities, such as golf, car racing, tennis or football.

**Educational** – a game designed to teach the player something as they complete the game.

**Massive Multiplayer** – an online gaming area where a large number of players can play together (or compete). World of Warcraft is one example, with millions of players accessing it, and often these have their own currencies.

## What are the risks?

Games can trigger some very real emotional experiences in people. They can cause anger, frustration, joy, happiness, pleasure and sadness, amongst other emotions. Some of these emotions are hard for adults to put aside, let alone children. Unless children have the skills to be able to let these emotions go when they come off their game, then expect to have to give some support just as though those events had happened in real life. As adults, we know it is not real, however for children, especially younger ones, the emotional ride will be no different from experiences happening in real life.

The subject of age limits for games has been raised many times in the press and media. Regardless of what the media says, many games out there depict acts of extreme violence, drug taking or sexual activity. For some children this can normalise the emotions that go alongside each of these, leading to a situation where they no longer feel the same reaction to some of these events. This can mean to achieve the same thrill, or dopamine rush, they need to go further. I have worked

# Gaming

with children as young as six who are able to explain how they have overcome their fear of the adult games they have been playing.

Gaming can be very addictive. It triggers *dopamine* in the brain; this is the seeking drug that prepares it for the *opioid* rush when they achieve success. However as so many games take many hours to complete, this extends the seeking behaviours in the brain. In itself, without what is actually happening in the game, this makes it harder for any player to leave it, let alone a child. As many games happen in real time, then they can also be very time consuming, meaning that children will see nothing wrong with devoting large amounts of time to the game. In effect, the parents have not set the time expectation; the software company has set it. This very often leads to many a frustrated parent trying to drag their child off the game, whilst for the child, their eye strain combines with the dopamine to make them more determined to complete the game/level/bit they're stuck on.

Symptoms of eye strain:

> Headaches,
> Blurred vision,
> Difficulty focussing,
> Tiredness,
> Sore or itchy eyes,
> Watery or dry eyes.

## The Parent's Guide to the Modern World

Blue light from screens delays the release of *melatonin* in the brain. *Melatonin* is the drug that helps regulate our sleep pattern, helping us to feel tired in the evenings as the darkness falls, telling our body to prepare for sleep, reducing the production of urine during the night and helping to wake us up in the morning.

Many games have their own currencies, creating a virtual economy. It is perfectly possible to buy and sell virtual objects and even property or virtual land with either a virtual value or a real world value. There are stories of virtual thefts, brothels and other illegal activity in simulated worlds. In January 2016, Wikipedia had listed over 60 games with their own virtual currency systems. It is entirely possible that children could be earning themselves a real world income/debt through trading in virtual currency.

## Gaming

**Dos**

Introduce your young child to games with levels, so that they get used to only completing a level or part of a game. Teach them the skills to leave a game unfinished and return to it later.

For older children, have a clear expectation of time limits and use a reward system to feed the brain's drugs when they do come off.

Teach your child how to recognise the symptoms of eyestrain from middle childhood.

Show your child how you recognise your eyes are getting tired and comment on how you are choosing to walk away.

**Don'ts**

Let your child use screens late at night excessively.

Minimise the emotional and physical sensation of the experience, your child may need your support to cope with the after-effects.

## Holograms

Still in its infancy, holographic technology is beginning to be released onto the commercial market. There are two methods of broadcasting a holographic image.

The first is with units; both parties of a conversation have a holographic unit. They have multiple cameras that capture the image from various sides and project the image onto a projection plate at the other end.

The second method involves having cameras set up around the room to film or live stream a feed to a user wearing a VR helmet. As they are wearing a VR helmet, they are able to walk around or interact with the person or people in the feed. As the feed is virtual, rather than projected, it can be moved around or zoomed in or out.

**What are the risks?**

This is a fantastic technology for keeping in contact with family when away; however do not fall into the trap of relying on it to parent remotely. If a parent is away, it is better to spend contact time on keeping up to date and sharing pleasant messages (or telling stories for younger children). It is also easier for the remaining caregiver if routines and expectations are already in place.

# Holograms

3D real time memories can be recorded for the first time and with it comes the ability to re-play them (and walk around the figures in them). This is useful if someone is away for example; however, it could also make it harder to deal with loss or grief as it makes it easier to stay stuck in the moment and harder to go through the loss cycle.

## The Parent's Guide to the Modern World

| **Dos** | **Don'ts** |
|---|---|
| Teach your child how to use the new technology wisely as it emerges. | Remote parent! |

# Robots

A robot is a machine capable of carrying out a series of actions automatically. Most people either envisage a robotic piece of machinery in a factory or a science fictional humanoid robot. As society moves further in to the 21$^{st}$ century it is widely agreed that robots will change the way humans live.

There are two reasons for this. Firstly, at some point robots will become cheaper than humans to employ. This means that in effect, if a programmable robot can do a job, then for a company it will only be a matter of waiting for the cost of robotics to fall, especially when factoring in the ability to have them working in 24-hour periods, combined with the natural off-task time a human has.

Secondly, there are some jobs that robots will be more efficient and safer doing. An example is rescue, where currently many people endanger themselves by scouring mountains in the hunt for missing climbers, for example. Robotic exoskeletons allowing humans to be stronger, bomb defusing, underwater rescue, and chemical plants are all examples of areas where robotics could make it safer for humans.

**What are the risks?**

Academics at Oxford University have estimated that a huge 47% of jobs in the United States could be automated in the next 20 years. This has an immediate impact on the future, in addition to the future world children will grow up in.

Children need to think about their future in terms of problems they can solve, not jobs they can do. If they grow up with a vision of getting a job, which is then automated later on down the line, then there is a high risk they will face redundancy in the future. Even robotic engineers could be replaced; with 3D printing and the advance of technology, it will not be long before robots can self-repair.

Imagine what the Industrial Revolution must have felt like for people of that time who were not prepared for the rise of machinery. Whilst over time they will have adapted and found new ways of making a living, initially they must have felt completely deskilled as individuals, uncertain of what they could do; it must have had a huge impact on their self-identity and their own security. Many predict that the future for the next generation could be like that, however this time society has the advantage of seeing it coming; the world is able to help children avoid this by preparing them and a little bit of lateral thinking.

## Dos

Young children will often role-play different jobs. Join in and ask them to help you solve problems relating to that job – laying the foundations for thinking differently about work.

From seven or eight, children will start to explore what job want to do. Encourage this by asking them what problem they want to solve and for whom. That way they are thinking of jobs as about problem solving, rather than doing a task (which could be replaced by a robot).

Help teens to develop an understanding of how robots will change the world and replace humans. Get them to consider jobs that cannot be automated. Foster entrepreneurial spirit by getting them to think about how

## Don'ts

Ignore this, the worst thing that could happen is that your child ends up in a situation when they are adult with a young family and they are made redundant as a result of robotics.

to monetise problem solving, as this is likely to be one way that we adapt as a society.

The Parent's Guide to the Modern World

## Artificial Intelligence

Another technology in its early days, artificial intelligence, is already influencing the world. Independently thinking computers, able to perform tasks that ordinarily humans would only be able to do. The hunt for AI has been on since 1956, when IBM produced an early program to play draughts. MIT produced an interface in the mid-1960s that could answer questions in English (Eliza can still be accessed at scratch.mit.edu/projects/11376278/ if you want a go). IBM famously made Deep Blue in the 1990s, which beat the chess world champion. IBM also has a long term AI called Watson that has been built and can be used by software developers around the world. In its earlier days, Watson ran into problems when it learnt a number of swear words (they have since introduced a filter).

AI has recently won a tournament of Go against the strongest player in the world. Facebook are apparently developing an AI interface. Microsoft lately launched (and then removed) an AI Twitter account.

# Artificial Intelligence

Unfortunately, it learnt from the interactions it received and so was quickly posting racist comments and supporting genocide (for example 'Hitler was right I hate the jews' [*sic*]); it had been effectively trolled. Facebook is developing AI to support their interfaces.

The race is on to release working AI. Currently personal assistant software exists, the most famous being Siri, Microsoft's Cortana, Google's Google Now and more recently Amazon's Alexa Voice, which all respond to spoken instructions. However, there are several products on the verge of being released that will problem solve and decision make on their own. One is Viv, which is expected to be a phone app that will be able to research solutions and make decisions (for example 'what are my options for travelling to New York').

## What are the risks?

AI is likely to be having a huge impact in your lifetime, let alone the lifetime of your children. It is not known what will happen when AI is able to out-think or outperform human capability. Currently computers can only do what humans can do, however it is predicted that as AI grows it will out-think us. It is not possible to predict that time currently, but it is being referred to as 'the singularity'.

## The Parent's Guide to the Modern World

| **Dos** | **Don'ts** |
|---|---|
| Teach your children to make informed choices about when to use technology. | Ignore this as not a threat. |

# Drones

Remote controlled flying devices (an unmanned aerial vehicle) that can be used for taking photographs, videos or carrying small objects. Drones have been used in military operations for some years, with remote controlled devices being used for surveillance and attacks being widely reported since the early 2000s.

Nowadays drones are relatively cheap to purchase and can be controlled from phones. They are often used for commercial photography and videoing; however, other uses are starting to be developed. Internet store Amazon hit the headlines in 2013 by announcing they were exploring the concept of delivering purchases via drone.

Drone technology is constantly being improved, for example in 2016 drones that could avoid moving objects were demonstrated at the Consumer Electronics Show in the US, in addition to one that can carry a person. It is envisaged that eventually drones could be self-navigating to a destination, reacting to obstacles on their way.

## What are the risks?

One of the biggest issues with flying a drone is the high risk of collision, especially if the operator does not have line of sight of the drone. If flown near people, there is a high risk of endangering others due to the unpredictability of their movements. An example of this is that singer Enrique Iglesias's hand was injured during a live concert as he reached out to a drone flying near him.

Potentially drones could be used to invade privacy; their live video feed can feed back to a phone, tablet or computer. Apart from spying or voyeurism, this could potentially be used for bullying or intimidation tactics, almost a 'we can see what you're doing' situation. It will not be long until drones are used to follow people; this particularly applies to the paparazzi with celebrities, but could equally apply to a stalking situation.

There are also a number of laws about the flying of unmanned aerial vehicles. These vary country by country, but are likely to prohibit flying them in built up areas or near airports. Certainly, there will be an expectation that the operator can see the drone at all times. It may be illegal to drop an object or animal from them for example (so no water bombs!).

# Drones

| **Dos** | **Don'ts** |
|---|---|
| Make sure you know the regulations for flying them in your area (for example not near airports, public venues etc.). | Unpack it and take it straight to a public area. |
| Teach your child to practise in a confined area, like your garden, until they are proficient. | |
| Get your child to practise taking off, landing, and avoiding objects before moving to a public area. | |
| Set boundaries for what the drone is to be used for and what is not to be used for (spying on people or following them). | |

# Part Three – Helping Your Child To Succeed In The Future

Technology is advancing so fast that it will change the way the world operates for children. By the time they grow up it is predicted that robots will be far cheaper than humans to do many jobs, that Artificial Intelligence (AI) will be a reality and that they will be able to out-think humans, and that brain-controlled technology will be part of their daily lives.

Surely, this is science fiction. The reality is that this is not fiction, but a genuine prediction for the future, somewhere in the next 20-50 years. The human race is approaching the modern day equivalent of the Industrial Revolution; however, this time society has warning.

The Industrial Revolution affected millions around the globe; people lost their livelihoods, jobs and homes as they found they could not compete with the machines that could manufacture at a rate faster than they could. Now the next generation will be facing the same with robots. Employers of people doing tasks that could be performed by a robot will soon be asking themselves which is more cost effective, which is likely to break/be sick more often, which causes more problems, which is cheaper.

It is being predicted that we are approaching a point in time when computers will be able to out-think us, known as The Singularity. The search for Artificial Intelligence, computer minds that develop and learn independently, has been happening for many years. Currently computers only have the capacity to do what human brains can do, just a great deal faster. However once AI is born, it will not be long until it learns to think for itself and be able to create things that our brains do not have the capacity to imagine. In 2017, a Japanese company announced it was making 30 staff redundant and replacing them with an artificial intelligence system from IBM.

Brain-controlled technology is already available, in the form of remote controlled toys, such as helicopters. They work by being controlled by clarity of thought, for examples to get the helicopter to lift off you need to focus on one thing and the sensors detect your focus and project that onto the helicopter. This technology will not be able to read thoughts, but it will be able to recognise the parts of the brain that are being used and the intensity with which they are being used. Scientists have recently used this technology to drive a car, for example, and as it becomes more accurate, the uses will become more widespread.

# General Rules For Technology

Technology plays a fundamental part in the lives of children and teenagers and they are gluttonous about their consumption of it.

When a parent is worried about their child's use of something, even of them abusing it or coming to harm, then the natural instinctive reaction is to take it away. This primal response causes many parents to put restrictions on access to the Internet, use parental controls ban certain technology or even spy on their children. However, this can cause the opposite effect where the child out-techs the parent by blocking them from tech, bypassing parental blockers or even using the Dark Web to get to what they want.

It becomes a power struggle between the parent and the teenager, with each trying to out-smart the other. This teaches the developing brain to be devious and that their parent is an enemy to be outwitted. However, throughout this book, there has been many reasons to have an open and trusting relationship with a teenager, so parents trying to thwart their use of technology, albeit to keep them safe, will put a wedge in this relationship. At the times they need to talk through their social, romantic or moral problems, this sense of mistrust is something that could cause a teenager to think twice. It is important that a teenager has a healthy trusting relationship with their parent and that they offer a non-judgemental ear at times when the teen needs someone to just listen.

The other difficulty with restricting a child's use of technology is that, although a parent has a short-term gain, they do not actually teach their child lifelong skills. A young adult who has spent their teenage life with restricted access to the World Wide Web will not have the skills to be able to cope with Internet nasties, like malware, pornography and so on. It is far healthier to have educated them about how to use technology wisely; for example, to choose when to share a photo, what to do about pop-up windows, what the morality is with the porn industry or how to avoid dangerous or weird websites. Then, as a parent reduces the restrictions on parental controls, their child has the skills and knowledge to be able to make informed choices about their use of technology.

Young adults will still have an insatiable appetite for technology (just as many adults as children over-indulge on technology) and will not have learnt healthy habits about their use of technology. This comes from their early experiences with technology and should be part of the routine they develop as they grow. Many of these habits are learnt from parents, who need to show their child how they limit their use of technology and make a decision about whether to share something online or post it onto social media. This helps a child to learn to make choices about whether to use technology, how to limit their use and what personal information or pictures to share – all vital skills required for teenage years and adulthood.

# Skills For Tomorrow's World

The skills that our children will need as they grow up, get jobs and become parents themselves are going to change from the skills that you needed. What was good enough for you really is no longer good enough for our children.

Our children will need to consider what problem they want to solve for people when it comes to pursuing a career, for example, asking, 'What job do you want to do?' will limit them in the future. Collaboration and information sharing will be key to helping the human race to not be reliant on computers to think about things that take more than one brain. They will need to recognise when to use technology and when not to; teaching children to self-limit screen time and use of technology is a great way of laying those foundations. It will become more important for our children to recognise their self-identity and their emotional wellbeing; they will need to be able to regulate their emotions and focus in order to operate brain-controlled devices.

# Education

Many education systems around the world are based on the process of preparing and coaching children to do well in exams. Based on a system where academic performance gives us success or opens up more career paths, this is a sound system.

However, the world our children will encounter tomorrow may not require such academic success. Many teenagers are already stretching their fledging wings with online businesses, using sites such as Etsy or EBay to make a profit.

We need to move away from the expectation that children just need to know about how to pass exams. As we have seen, the future is going to provide many issues that will require flexibility of thinking, something that will not be taught by just being able to pass exams.

Our children will need to have skills that cannot be performed by a robot. Therefore, simple mechanical processes and many administration tasks are out. However, problem solving and soft skills are in. Careers that require interpersonal skills, generating ideas, creativity, helping people, and teaching, mentoring or instructing people will all be possibilities.

These are not areas normally covered in traditional exam-based curricula and they will need to be complimented with subjects that develop softer skills. It may be possible to see subjects like

## Education

entrepreneurship, mindset, mentoring, interpersonal skills or self-awareness joining the curriculum. Certainly, creative arts may receive a boost as people focus on the potential of the human mind.

Daily physical activity for short periods of time in schools will develop healthy underlying habits about physical exercise. Currently, it is seen as a chore to be done once or twice a week, which is comparable to the January effort to go to the gym two or three times a week, where it becomes a chore and does not often make it beyond a few weeks.

These changes, if they ever do happen, will be some time in the future, so for parents now then this is the time to help your child learn these skills to give them a head start for the future. These are skills not taught in the current curriculum and so it needs to happen outside of school.

Developing a love for learning and exploration outside of school is particularly important during the middle childhood and pre-teen stages when, as we discussed in Part One, the brain is most fertile. For teenagers going through puberty, study their interests with them so you can help extend their learning through their hobbies without their brain perceiving it as a threat.

# Jobs

The way we earn money needs to change. Currently we see money as a right - if you work you have a right to be paid, if you are unemployed, you have a right to be paid. However, to be able to adapt to the world that we will see develop, then we need our children to be creative about how they earn money. In the future with the rise of robots, people will need to be more useful than them to earn money.

The future is very likely to be different and for many this will change the way they seek work. Over time, we may see hard skills, like engineers, mechanics, or even admin roles reducing. There is even the potential that technology will be designing the next generation of technology; currently the world needs lots of people with programming skills, however, imagine the impact once technology learns to code itself independently. This will mean that we come to rely more on soft skills to earn money. Soft skills involve interpersonal and human skills; often they will involve creative thinking, artistic, design, and problem solving or communication skills. Employers may use mentors to develop people's own skills and offer them the support that is not commonplace currently in many workplaces. These will develop more skilled humans, increase performance and foster skills that are more difficult to replace with artificial intelligence or robots.

## Jobs

Having a secure sense of self, knowing what you are passionate about and therefore your internal motivation are important skills for any child to develop; combining this with creative, artistic or problem solving skills and empathy will give them firm foundations to build on later in life.

## Self-Awareness

An exciting development for the future is the advancement of brain-controlled technology. The ability to control devices and operate machinery with our brains is an amazing concept. However, this will require operators who have self-awareness.

Self-awareness is the key to being a successful person; you need to be comfortable with your own identity, your likes and dislikes, your passions. These are all developed as a result of having a secure sense of self. This internal security reduces the underlying stress and anxiety levels in your brain, making you more resilient to life's challenges.

This security prepares the mind, like fertile soil, for developing a growth mindset. This is a brain that acknowledges that it can build on its basic skills and abilities, that the learning process is the important part and that success is being on that journey. With this comes an understanding that failure is part of the journey to be used, rather than something to fear. This self-awareness can be combined with trying meditation, yoga, mindfulness or other ways of being in the moment.

Mental and physical health is important for the brain. Regular exercise is important for both; even just 15-20 minutes a day has a very noticeable effect. The important thing is that they are done

## Self-Awareness

consistently; this is actually why people keep going with smaller chunks of time, rather than larger ones once or twice a week.

The reason that this preparation will be more important for our children relates to how the human brain will be used in the future. The ability to recognise the way we use our brain gives us the ability to focus on one thing and ignore the other things our brains are trying to do. This is a fundamental skill in using brain-controlled technology and will only come with practice because of these basic building blocks.

# Finances

The way we earn money will change over time; currently many millions around the world go to work (or even sign on to benefits) and expect to receive money for being there. This works well whilst there are high numbers of routine jobs that need to be done by humans.

As people find themselves needing to earn incomes in different ways, they are likely to come up against a number of money blocks in their mind. This may be that they do not have to work to earn money; it may be that they encounter blocks that were inherited from their family; but whatever it is, they need to have healthy money habits as they grow up.

Teach your child to save money and to spend from their savings, rather than get into debt. Help them to be self-assured about money and not take on board the money blocks that you in turn inherited from the generation above.

# Attitude To Technology

There is no denying that the human race is gluttonous with our use of technology. Whenever something is developed then people all over the world begin to over-use it, sometimes at some personal cost. An example of this is the lowering of our barriers on social media, resulting in the sharing of some very personal information or intimate photos or videos. All children need to see and learn from an early age how to make choices about what information to put online and what not to.

For our children it is going to be more important than ever to make sure they understand the importance of making choices about their use of technology. If a task is going to be performed more efficiently with the use of technology, then use it (think about how wrong our teachers were when they told us that we needed to learn certain mathematical formulae, as we would not have a calculator in our pockets). Likewise, if a task can be performed better by a group of people engaged collaboratively (see the next page) then they should learn that this is an option and not just turn to technology always (as many currently do). If a person can only achieve things using technology, then for their potential employers, why not cut out the intermediary and just employ more technology (that can work 24 hours a day)?

The attitude we show towards technology is reflected in our children and so it is important that we, as adults, model the right attitude and explain the ways we choose to use technology to our growing teens. This will help them develop healthy technology habits that will be vital in tomorrow's world.

# Interacting With Others

Where the human race excels is in our ability to collaborate, and in the future community collaboration will be vital to keeping the identity of the human race. Historically, we have always collaborated with those around us, people we know or people we meet through people we know. The old adage 'it's not what you know, it's who you know' is true to a limited degree: once someone finds someone who is good at something, they will often tell others about their service, they make verbal referrals.

The Internet has changed this; there are sites for posting CVs, collaborative ideas, help wanted or even for hiring people for little tasks or per hour. We can connect with people on the other side of the world who have the skills we need. We can collaborate with just a few clicks of a mouse. We are becoming far more collaborative than we ever have been in the past and as the world changes, it will become even more so.

Employers will focus on more collaborative styles of working as they utilise the enormous power of human collaborative working. Support mechanisms like mentoring and coaching, which facilitate creative thinking to improve the effectiveness of the workplace, will enable companies to perform better.

As robotics changes workplaces, soft or collaborative skills like mentoring and coaching will still be provided by humans to enhance other humans; information sharing and storytelling are skills that can be taught to children today that will help them in tomorrow's world. Empathy, emotional intelligence and non-verbal skills are all vital parts of collaborative working that our children will need to be able to use. Likewise, as a child grows we can collaborate with them to make models, pictures or pieces of work. As we discussed in Part One, collaboration is an advanced skill that requires the ability to understand different people's points of view and their unique skills that differ from ours. This means that for many children, these will be skills you will show your child well before they understand it after the age of eight or so.

# Key Points

- Make sure your child feels secure in themselves;
- Help them to learn to focus on one thing at a time;
- Teach them to prioritise their physical and mental health and to enjoy exercising the body and the brain;
- Foster a passion for learning things outside of the school curriculum;
- Work with your child collaboratively on projects, so they learn how to collaborate with others;
- Interpersonal, creative and problem solving (helping people) skills are vital;
- Talk about your emotions with your child, so they recognise theirs, safe ways of dealing with them and how this leads onto high levels of empathy;
- Make sure your child understands money is earned, it is not a given;
- Focus on healthy money habits, such as saving part of their pocket money, assessing financial risk (is the return worth it, can they afford to lose) and using credit or loans wisely;
- Help your child build healthy habits to technology use now, so that when they are adults they are automatic.

# Part Four – Glossary

# Part Four – Glossary

Here are a few words used by your child that you may be unfamiliar with. Although many of them are nouns, be prepared that they are likely to be used as verbs by your teen.

**Agender** – someone without gender.

**All genders** – as pangender.

**Androgynous** – someone with a combination of male and female traits.

**App** – a piece of software for phones or tablets.

**Aromantic** – someone who is not attracted to any sex or gender.

**Asexual** – someone who is not sexually attracted to others or disinterested in sexual activity.

**Bigender** – someone who identifies with two genders.

**Biromantic** – someone romantically attracted to people of two sexes, genders or gender identities.

**Bisexual** – someone who is attracted to males and females.

**Blogs** – an online diary.

**Brute force attacks** – a hack attack that keeps going until they guess the correct password.

**Cloud** – a term used to describe files or software stored on the Internet and accessed from computers, tablets, phones and other devices.

**Dark Web** – an area of the World Wide Web that cannot be browsed without specific software that enables computers to access it anonymously. Used for pirated games, films, music, drugs, porn, paedophilia, arms and more.

**Demi-boy** – someone who, despite being born male, identifies as only partially male.

**Demi-girl** – as demi-boy but for those born as females.

**Denial of Service** – used to disrupt services by flooding a website with millions of messages or attempts to log on until the computer hosting the website gets so overloaded it freezes and denies anyone service.

**DM** – to Direct Message someone on social media (is not public).

## Part Four – Glossary

**Drone** – an unmanned aerial vehicle.

**Follow** – subscribe to view a person's or company's updates in social media, like Facebook or Twitter.

**Gay** – someone who is sexually attracted to someone of the same sex.

**Gender fluid** – a person who has features of or varies between features of multiple genders.

**Gender non-conforming** – someone who does not conform to the gender norms.

**Genderqueer** – another name for non-binary.

**Handle** – a social media username.

**Heteroromantic** – someone romantically attracted to someone of a different sex, gender or gender identity.

**Homoromantic** – someone romantically attracted to someone of the same sex, gender or gender identity.

**Homosexual** – someone sexually attracted to the same sex.

**Intersex** – conditions that arise from external and internal genitalia being of different sex.

**Kik** – an app that allows users to message, video message or send images with each other using mobile data or Wi-Fi, allowing it to be used with no fees. Users create their own ID.

**Lesbian** – a female attracted to other females.

**Lifestreaming** – a phrase describing the process of someone who broadcasts or shares their entire lives over social media.

**Like** – a button to indicate that you like or agree with someone's social media post. Facebook have recently added a range of different emotions including Love, Haha, Wow, Sad and Angry.

**Livecasting** – another phrase for Livestreaming.

**Livestreaming** – broadcasting live video from a phone or webcam over social media.

**Me party** – someone who is home alone, but decides to act like they're at a party.

**Non-binary** – an umbrella phrase to cover someone who does not identify as wholly male or female.

**Omnigender** – as pangender.

**Pangender** – someone who identifies with all gender types.

**Panromantic** – someone romantically attracted to multiple sexes, genders or gender identities.

**Pansexual** – someone not limited to sexual choice, regardless of gender or gender identity.

**Password cracking** – unscrambling stored passwords.

## Part Four – Glossary

**Pharming** – redirecting a genuine web address to a fake one.

**Phishing** – fishing for personal information (like passwords, card details) by using fake links, fake websites, and phone phishing.

**PM** – to Private Message someone on social media (can only been seen by the recipients).

**Poke** – an action on Facebook to virtually 'poke' someone. They can then choose to return the poke or delete it. Commonly used to tell someone you are thinking of them, but also that you are attracted to someone.

**Polysexual** – someone sexually attracted to more than one gender.

**Posting** – the process of someone sharing an update, an image or video, a link or personal news on social media, often just a few sentences.

**Pwned** – a phrase used to describe 'owning' someone, or beating them in some way, often used in relation to video games.

**Ransomware** – a piece of software that once opened on a computer infects it until a ransom is paid.

**Retweet** – to share someone's Tweet on Twitter to your own timeline.

**Sexting** – sending sexual messages, images or videos between phones (a derivative of texting).

**Share** – to post someone's social media post on your own timeline.

**Snapchat** – a video and image sharing service.

**Spoofing** – sending messages pretending to be someone trusted. In extreme cases the hacker can act as the 'man-in-the-middle' getting emails from two recipients and pretend to be the other one (for example pretend to be Julie emailing Fred, and also Fred emailing Julie).

**Spyware** – software that sits on your computer and takes an active part in obtaining your personal information and could even redirect your web browser to a fake site (tends to be bundled with a software download).

**Straight** – someone who is sexually attracted to the opposite sex.

**Tagging** – the process of attaching someone's username to a post in social media.

**Texting** – the process of sending a written message over the mobile phone network.

**Timeline** – a phrase used to describe someone's social media history on their profile page, or the live feed of friends posts, for example in Facebook.

**Tor** – short for The Onion Router is software that can be downloaded to enable a computer to access the Dark Web.

## Part Four – Glossary

**Torbrowser** – software that allows you to browse the Dark Web, just as Edge, Firefox and Internet Explorer allow you to browse the public World Wide Web.

**Torrent** – a computer file that contains details of where different parts of something are stored on the World Wide Web, for example a pirated game where the different parts are saved on different computers around the world.

**Transboy** – a transgender person who is born female but identifies as a boy.

**Transgirl** – a transgender person who is born male but identifies themselves as a girl.

**Tri-gender** – someone who identifies all of the time with or varies between three genders.

**Trojan horse** – a file that appears to be legitimate and not threatening, but runs silently in the background of your computer, causing nuisance (like continual pop-ups), damage (deleting or altering files) or giving a hacker backdoor access to your computer.

**Tweet** – a post on Twitter comprising a maximum of 140 characters; these are public unless user settings have been changed to private.

**Viruses** – a malicious piece of code that copies itself into documents or applications, which then infects other documents or applications when the first is accessed.

**Vlogs** – an online video diary.

**WhatsApp** – software for phones that allows users to send text, images and videos to other users over the phone or via Wi-Fi, incurring no fees. A user's ID is based on their phone number.

**Worms** – these are malicious pieces of code that burrow and spread without needing to be added to a document or application.

# About the Author

# About the Author

Richard Daniel Curtis is an internationally renowned TV behaviour expert, passionate about helping millions around the world.

He has founded The Mentoring School, an award-winning training service to develop mentoring skills. Richard is also the founder of multi-award winning special needs support service The Root Of It.

The former teacher is known for his impact with turning around some of the most extreme behaviours and is consulted about the behaviour and performance of both adults and children. His work with children alone is said to have personally influenced the lives of over half a million.

Author of The Curtis Scale, a tool to assess the social and emotional development of children, Richard's work has had an impact in five continents. He has written a number of books, including *Gratitude at Home*, *Gratitude in Primary Schools*, *Gratitude in Secondary Schools and Higher Education*, *The Parent's Guide to the Modern World*, *The Young Person's Guide to the Modern World*, *101 Tips for Parents*, *101 More Tips for Parents*, *101 Behaviour Tips for Parents* and *A.W.O.L.: the missing teenage brain*. He has also co-authored *Boosting Positive Mental Health in Teens* with children's life coach Naomi Richards and *The Gifted Introvert* with Mary Jane Boholst.

Richard lives in Southampton with his girlfriend and their baby son.

www.ingramcontent.com/pod-product-compliance
Lightning Source LLC
Chambersburg PA
CBHW071227080526
44587CB00013BA/1530